GO

Sir Harry Secombe, CBE was born in Swansea in 1921. After a spell as a pay clerk, he joined the Territorial Army and saw action in Sicily, Italy and North Africa, met Spike Milligan, and developed an interest in entertainment. Demobbed in 1946, he made his first professional stage appearance at the Windmill Theatre. Radio breaks followed, then came the celebrated *Goon Show*, television shows, variety theatre, films and musicals. He contributes regularly to a number of magazines, especially *Punch*.

His novels, *Twice Brightly* and *Welsh Fargo*, are also available in Fontana.

GOON ABROAD

Harry Secombe

Illustrations by the author

Fontana/Collins

First published in Great Britain by
Robson Books 1982
First issued in Fontana Paperbacks 1983

Copyright © Harry Secombe 1982

Thanks are due to the editors and proprietors of the
following publications in which some of these pieces
originally appeared: *Punch*, *High Life*, *Daily Telegraph Magazine*, *Daily Mirror*, *Sunday Times*, *Sticky
Wickets* (The Lord's Taverners). 'Games' was first
published in a copyright collection, *Up With Skool*,
and appears by permission of Penguin Books; 'Tony
Hancock' was written as a preface to *Tony Hancock:
Artiste* published by Eyre Methuen.

Phototypesetting by Georgia Origination, Liverpool
Made and printed in Great Britain by
William Collins Sons & Co. Ltd, Glasgow

Contents

Foreword

When I decided to call this collection of pieces *Goon Abroad*, I meant 'abroad' in the sense of being out and about. It so happens that quite a few of these concern my adventures in various parts of the world, but it is not supposed to be a book about travel. There are plenty of those about, God knows. I just thought I'd put the record straight, that's all. No point in searching these pages for tales of derring-do in foreign parts. As they say about a certain Sunday newspaper – 'All of human life is here'. Well, not *all*, but the odd gleanings from the factory floor of life. Find out for yourself or put it back on the shelf. And take your gloves off.

Harry Secombe

Goon Down Memory Lane

Beginnings

WE WOULD LIE in bed, my brother and I, listening to the sounds of the ships' sirens, and dream our separate dreams. Fred always wanted to be a missionary from the time he was very small, and I intended to be the strongest man in the world. In another room my sister lay, mentally walking hospital corridors, a shining vision in white, while my parents just lay in bed wondering what would become of us all.

From the time I was four we lived in a council house in St. Thomas, Swansea, on an estate which overlooked the docks and the L.M.S. railway sidings. Behind us was a large recreation ground and from the safety of our iron railings we could watch the strivings of our local football and cricket teams. Vicarious sportsmen, my brother and I were never members of any of the sides. I was too short-sighted and too often stricken with childhood illnesses, and my brother was too busy studying for his role as a propagator of the Gospel in far-off lands. My father, who had played soccer, rugby and cricket at various times in his life, would explain the finer details of the games to us. 'See, now, boys, if Charlie Thomas had not tripped the referee when Glyn Evans was about to kick Jackie Griffiths in the face, the goal scored by Sammy Thomas, who was really offside at the time, would have been disallowed.'

The jerseys of the teams were never regulation and it was difficult to tell which side was defending which goal. An uncle of mine, wearing his own football jersey, once scored four goals for St. Stephen's Athletic before they found out that he was only a spectator. Fortunately for St. Stephen's the goals were not disallowed because it was discovered that the opposing side had three extra forwards. They only found that out when at half-time the team manager was three pieces of lemon short.

I was never very keen on soccer – it was too complicated for me. But cricket – ah, cricket – I loved the game. I would watch eagerly from my bedroom window as Grenfell Park first eleven took the field – actually there were twelve. They had no dressing-rooms – the players would change into their whites or grey flannels on the boundary, and many a pleasantly-shocked clucking of tongues would come from behind half-drawn blinds as elderly ladies watched the shirt tails flapping in the breeze. It was lovely to lie in bed recovering from chickenpox and listen to the sound of bat on ball, and the occasional crash of glass as Bert Woodward opened his shoulders and hit old Mr. Orchard's greenhouse again.

We had little money to spare; sometimes it ran so low we would have to stoop to pick it up. But we had fun as a family and we were rich in affection for each other. My mother was really the head of the family although she always let my father think that he was. 'Wait until your father comes home,' she would admonish us. 'Wait until

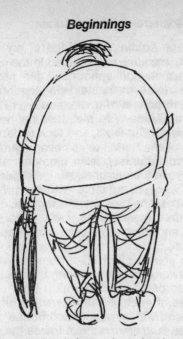

your mother gets back from shopping,' my father would say, hiding behind his paper.

We were a strong church-going family, too. My brother and I were in the choir at St. Thomas Church from the time that we were seven years of age. For a long time, owing to the fact that I was so short, myself and David Porter – who was even shorter – led the choir from the vestry. It was quite a big church, built in 1860-odd in Welsh Gothic style, and had very beautiful stained glass windows through which shafts of light would shine upon the choir stalls on summer Sunday evenings, and I would bathe self-consciously in them. I would listen with apparent concentration to the droning sermon – all the time aware of Mildred Jones watching me from the second pew and hoping that she could not see the piece

13

of adhesive tape holding the bridge of my spectacles together. Then, when the vicar turned in the pulpit at the end of the sermon and announced the next hymn, I would leap smartly to my feet and sing loudly and clearly if it happened to be one of my favourites. I would throb with emotion in 'Abide With Me', toss my head gaily in 'Now Thank We All Our God', and look suitably parched in 'As Pants The Hart For Cooling Streams'. The choirmaster-cum-organiser, from his commanding view of the choirboys in the mirror above the organ keyboard, used to say that I could put more into 'Rock of Ages' with my face than the whole of the Morriston Orpheus with their two hundred male voices. I was also capable of hanging on to an 'Amen' until both myself and the vicar had gone purple.

There was a great sigh of relief from the whole of the choir when my voice began to change. I was transferred to pumping the organ, a task which I performed with varying degrees of energy. The trick of pumping was to watch a little lead weight suspended from a cord which was attached to some mechanism inside the organ, and which moved above and below a mark pencilled on the side of the instrument. If the weight went above the mark you had to pump the wooden handle like mad to keep the air going and bring the weight down again. Below it, you were safe. I remember one very warm evening falling asleep during the sermon on my little bench behind the organ. The vicar had finished his sermon and declared that the next hymn would be 'Fight The Good Fight'. The organist, head back, and pedalling furiously, pounded out the first few chords with majestic grandeur then wailed to a stop like a punctured set of bagpipes. I was subsequently put on to painting the drainpipes outside the vestry.

Christmas Eve used to be great fun for the choir. We would all go down to the Seamen's Mission at the docks and sing carols for them. One Christmas when it came to my turn to sing 'Silent Night', I curled up and died inside as the clear treble I had delivered at practice degenerated into an uncertain croak. My brother, who suffered almost as much as I did on these occasions, put his hand to his eyes. I was mesmerised by the mass of faces before me and suddenly, in a desperate attempt to hide, I snatched off my glasses. The result was most comforting – I could not distinguish anything in front of me, and with a new confidence I sang the rest of my solo as if to myself. Since then I have always performed without my spectacles – the illusion, to a very short-sighted person like myself, of being removed from the rest of the world, is most welcome, especially on a big empty stage facing a big empty audience.

My father would do a turn at these concerts, always unwillingly. He would only perform his monologue – 'The Wreck of the 11.69' – if a chair was provided for him to put his foot on. If he kept his knees apart there was no danger of them knocking, and he could always hold on to the back of the chair for support. The real star of the family, though, was my sister Carol. From a very early age she displayed all the manifestations of future stardom. She was pretty and had a highly-developed sense of comedy. In all the local talent competitions she was always in the prize money, and I'm sure that if she had kept it up she would have done extremely well in the profession. She suddenly gave it all up during the war, for no apparent reason, and has no theatrical aspirations whatever today.

At one time she and I would do a version of a Welsh courtship which we had taken down verbatim from a record made by Ted and May Hopkins, the famous Welsh comedy team. I was merely the feed, but my knees would tremble violently and the old butterflies would start fluttering in my stomach for at least half an hour before we went on to perform. It was only after I had realised that I could be an ostrich without my glasses that I ever began to get any confidence. Later on I branched out into doing Stanley Holloway monologues and impersonations of Sandy Powell and Stainless Stephen.

Most of my father's side of the family were keen amateur performers. My Aunt Margery used to play the piano in Woolworth's in Swansea for years, and still plays piano in a local orchestra. Cyril, my father's brother, was a great inspiration to us all. He could play the musical saw. He used to get an ordinary saw, place it between his legs and get lovely soprano-like notes out of it by beating it with a large drumstick. How he managed to do so without inflicting serious injury upon himself I shall never know.

Then there was my Aunt Margery's husband, George Charles, who played drums for years with the 'Keskersays' band at the Langland Bay Hotel, and was also a fine tap dancer. He even taught me a few basic time steps which I remember to this day. We used to go into the garden of my grandparents' house in Williams Street and dance on a proper tap mat he had had since the days when was a pro himself. For hours he would try to teach me how to flick my foot to get that double tap sound, and I would hop about with all the grace of a penguin. They were happy days indeed.

'And that', to quote from Leslie Bricusse's lyric to Cyril Ornadel's musical version of *Pickwick*, 'is how it all began, Sam, that's how it all began.'

Swansea

TO TELEVISION VIEWERS upon whose retinas I am forever etched against a background of two hundred and fifty singing Welsh miners, it might come as a surprise to learn that I cannot speak Welsh. Indeed, in the dockland area of Swansea in which I was raised, we were more familiar with Asian dialects than with the language of the Cymru.

I was born in Dan-y-Graig Terrace, overlooking the docks, and when I was four the family moved to a house on a new council estate about half-a-mile away, but still within the sound of clanking steam engines and ships' sirens. Behind us loomed Kilvey Hill, over six hundred feet high, its bulk sheltering Swansea from the east wind and its slopes providing a playground for us children. I used to love to climb as far as the disused reservoir about half-way up and look out at the sweeping crescent of Swansea Bay stretching from Port Talbot to the Mumbles Head. To the west is Town Hill, separated from the east side of Swansea by the River Tawe which flows into the sea below Kilvey Hill, ushered on the last few hundred yards of its journey by two piers.

Down towards the bottom of the hill stands St. Thomas Church, the clock in its tower with its four black faces and its eight gold hands tyrannising the neighbourhood, its bells reproaching the ungodly a mile out to sea. A lean greyhound of a church looking down disdainfully from its eminence on the non-conformist terriers of Port Tennant Road.

Most of my childhood memories are centred around St. Thomas Church and its activities: choir practice, socials in the church hall, where my sister performed monologues and sketches in which I was at first an unwilling stooge until the acting bug got me. Whitsun treats provided great excitement. We would all gather on Whit Monday at the Midland Station and pile into gritty coaches for the long haul to Killay, about six miles away. It would inevitably rain when we arrived at the field, and the umbrellas would go up over the trestle tables piled with sandwiches and cakes and two large tea urns, with cups and saucers of thick china all marked 'St. Thomas Church'. A smell of wet grass and tea leaves and a faint hint of whisky from a church warden's breath. Three-legged races and egg-and-spoon races, and the prizes presented by the vicar with a brief smile and a wave of a pudgy hand. Then off home, scolded on to the train by tired teachers and parents, an apple and an orange in your pocket as a parting gift, and the vicar a church-warden short.

Saturday afternoon shopping with my mother was something that my brother and sister and I fought over. One of us would go with her to help carry home the groceries up the steep St. Ledger Crescent from the tram stop on Port Tennant Road. My mother was a great one for 'shop-window fuddling' as she called it. She would wander around the large stores – Ben Evans, David Evans, Lewis Lewis, Edwards Eagle – comparing prices, clicking her tongue as she handled the merchandise, and all the time behind her I would walk, wide-eyed at the goods on display, trailing the stout empty basket.

Swansea Market was an Aladdin's Cave in those days, and that was where we always headed eventually. At the main entrance in Oxford Street sat the Penclawdd cockle women in their shawls and hats; before them their tubs of cockles covered with spotless linen cloths, glass measures ready in their hands to serve the passing customer. Around the perimeter of the market were the butchers' and poulterers' shops with clean sawdust-covered floors. There were little cafés set into the wall where you sat at scrubbed tables and ate fresh faggots and peas. Laverbread, a special food made from seaweed and looking like cow pat, was always on sale in the market, along with little bags of oatmeal. My mother used to cook it for Sunday breakfast with bacon and there was no taste as delicious in all the world.

The body of the market was taken up with stalls of every kind. Mounds of home-made toffee, marshmallow mushrooms, boiled sweets in the shape of pineapples, pears, and even goldfish; sensible dresses hanging from hooks, leather footballs and football boots; chinaware, glassware and, pervading the whole building, the combined aroma of its wares.

My mother would slowly work her way through the stalls, the basket getting heavier now as she got down to the serious business of shopping for the weekend. 'Shwnies' from the valleys, speaking Welsh and wearing caps and scarves crossed at the neck and tucked into their waistcoats, would jostle shoulders good-naturedly with the tweed-suited gentlemen from Brynmill and Sketty, where the posh people came from. 'Lace curtains and no dinner' territory. Through the market now and into the Dolphin fish and chip shop opposite the stage-door of the Swansea Empire for a sit-down meal. My mother rubbing her hands to get the blood circulating in the weals caused by the string of the carrier bags. And me, the full basket at my feet, with my glasses all steamed up, tucking into a four-penny cutlet and two penn'orth. 'There's a good boy for your mother – eat up tidy.'

What I liked about the Swansea I knew in those early council house days was the warmth and friendship which surrounded us. The 'twenties and 'thirties were hard times, but there were compensations. In summer we had the whole of Gower to explore for the price of a ticket on the Mumbles train. Or, with our bathing costumes wrapped in towels and tucked under our arms, we could walk down to the beach for a dip.

As a family, we did not have much in the way of material possessions, but neither did any of our neighbours, and maybe that was our strength as a community.

I have confined myself to my childhood experiences in Swansea because to me they are more vivid than many subsequent happenings. Perhaps that is why I could never find that particular kind of happiness if I went back there to live. Many of the places I knew have disappeared to make way for new building projects; many were bombed during the war. Friends and relatives are scattered now, and I have felt an interloper on the odd occasions that I've visited the old council estate.

Yet I shall always love Swansea for two things. First, for a happy childhood, and second, for providing me with a wife.

I have never really left Swansea, I have taken it with me.

All I Want for Christmas . . .

WHEN I PLAYED the character Pickwick in the musical of the same name there was one scene early on in the piece in which I had to strut around the stage in a bald wig, weaving my way in and out of the chorus whilst singing a song which began 'Turkeys bigger than I am, snowflakes made of lace, that's what I'd like for Christmas . . .' My mind used to seize up at the thought of poultry weighing sixteen stone or more; I imagined the struggle to get it into the oven, cold turkey sandwiches continuing well into July. And snowflakes made of *lace*? It would be lovely for dressmakers to be able to nip out in a snowstorm and pick up material for wedding gowns off the street, but fancy being caught in a lace drift.

No, huge turkeys and lace snowflakes are definitely not what I would like for Christmas. Although the Christmas present I wanted above everything else in my life, and never got, was almost as big as I was. It was a gigantic Christmas stocking packed with goodies which

21

hung from wires in the window of a grocer's shop in Port Tennant Road, Swansea, when I was about seven years old.

I first noticed this Christmas present to end all Christmas presents when I was shopping with my mother. 'GRAND RAFFLE FOR THIS MAGNIFICENT STOCKING. TICKETS 3D EACH OBTAINABLE INSIDE. TO BE DRAWN ON CHRISTMAS EVE. FOR REGULAR CUSTOMERS ONLY' said a poster outside. I stood with my nose pressed against the shop window, looking upwards in awe at the glittering prize. It was so big that a large Cadbury's selection box fitted easily into the toe, and through the pink mesh of the stocking I could see incredible things like a Hornby train and a big torch and at least two Boys' Annuals. Other highly desirable items designed to drive a boy out of his mind were hinted at behind the holly and red ribbon which decorated the outside of the stocking. I remained transfixed at the window and was only removed by my mother after a prolonged struggle.

'Come on, Harry,' she said. 'We're not regular customers.' That did it.

When we got home I went into a decline, refusing to eat – a rare rebellion for me – and generally making a nuisance of myself. After a short debate my parents decided that perhaps if I behaved myself and came down off the roof they might consider registering as customers and buying a few raffle tickets. Win or lose, it was to be my Christmas present – I missed the heavy wink my father gave my mother. I became a model child from that moment on, being polite to my brother and sister, passing the sugar without spilling it, saying Please and Thank you – and generally making a nuisance of myself. All my pocket money went on tickets for the raffle and not a day went by without my face being pressed against the shop window. I was actually beginning to make an impression on the glass. I would check the contents of the stocking as well as I could to make sure that nothing had been removed, examine the Hornby train for signs of rust, and be in a constant fret that the chocolate in the selection box might melt before the draw.

I held twelve tickets in my hot sticky hand as I stood with my mother in the sawdust of the packed grocer's shop on Christmas Eve. They had put all the tickets in a biscuit tin covered with red paper, and a little girl was lifted on to the counter to make the draw. Why can't *I* pick the ticket? I thought. I could have found any one of my counterfoils without looking – I knew the numbers by feel. The little girl, simpering, rummaged around in the tin, helped on by cries of 'Pick mine! Pick mine!' I had a loud voice even then. She pulled out a crumpled pink slip and handed it to Mr. Roberts the grocer. Three of *my* tickets were pink. He straightened it out.

'The winning number for this wonderful Christmas prize is . . .' Mr. Roberts paused, taking full advantage of the occasion.

'Get on with it!' My mother put her hand over my mouth.

'One hundred and thirty-six!'

I didn't have to look. I knew all my numbers and that wasn't one of them. I wasn't even near it. No Hornby train, no selection box, no Boys' Annuals. Without waiting to see who had won I ran out of the shop and cried all the way home.

In my own stocking the following morning I had a watch with a luminous dial and a Boys' Annual and a torch with three different coloured heads, but it took me a long time to get over my disappointment.

As a matter of fact I'm *still* not over it. You can keep your Neiman Marcus super Christmas presents – His and Her Golf Clubs – Sunningdale for him and

Wentworth for her – eighteen-carat gold models of Battersea Power Station or whatever. I'd rather settle for that stocking in Roberts's window. The Hornby train alone would be worth a fortune now.

24

Games

IF ANYONE EVER asks me what my favourite subject was in school I always say 'Games'. That was the time I used to like best – when we were let out of the chalk-riddled atmosphere of the classroom into the fresh air of the playground. There was only one drawback – the surface of the yard was covered with asphalt, and every time we fell down it really hurt. To this day, if my memory fails me about my schooldays I just run my fingers over my knees or my elbows and the memories come flooding back as I feel there the scars I acquired playing soccer, rounders, cricket, leap-frog or rugby. Especially rugby, because I was brought up in Swansea, and any boy who did not play our national game was a 'cissy'.

I have to confess, though, that I was not very good at games. From the age of seven I had to wear spectacles to correct my short-sightedness and I was always afraid of getting them broken. It was pretty impossible to play without them, and so I always held back from tackling and would give up the ball very quickly when challenged. There was one day, though, when I actually scored a goal. This was when I had progressed to Dynevor Secondary School which boasted a grass playing-field and real goal posts, not coats placed apart on the ground.

We were playing another form at soccer, and I was right back. That was as far away from the action as I could get without actually being behind the goal mouth. As we were the third team, we had to take whatever jerseys were left over, and both sides wore a variety of colours.

I was dawdling near the touchline, talking to a friend who had come to see me play because he needed a laugh – his hamster had just died – when a horde of yelling lunatics descended on me and I found myself lying face down in the mud with my spectacles broken and both nostrils plugged with Welsh turf. The referee, our sports master, sent me back to the pavilion to try to sort myself out. My friend, who was now hysterical with laughter, came with me, his dead hamster forgotten. It was useless trying to repair my shattered glasses, and once I had cleared out my nose I decided to go back on to the field again, if only to get rid of my cackling companion.

I peered uncertainly about me as I took up the position I had left. All the other players were up the far end again, and I jumped up and down on the spot to keep warm. Suddenly, without warning, I found the ball at my feet. It had somehow been kicked all the way from the distant end of the pitch. Not knowing quite what to do, I began to dribble it in a somewhat desultory fashion towards the other goal. To my surprise I met with little resistance and with a pounding heart slammed the ball into the net. A goal!

I turned and squinted towards my fellow players,

expecting hands thudding congratulations on my back. Instead my captain rushed up to me shouting 'You fool, Secombe, you fool!'

'What d'you mean?' I said, puzzled. 'I've scored a goal.'

'It's an *own* goal,' screamed my captain. 'We changed sides for the second half when you were in the dressing-room'.

That was the last time I ever played soccer. I wasn't really sorry though. I was into cricket by the time Spring came around. You see, they needed a sight-screen.

Goon Out and About

Cheating

I, HARRY SECOMBE, ex-choir boy, brother of the Rector of Hanwell and late of the television programme 'Stars on Sunday', confess to having cheated several times in my life. There is no use pretending any more. I have worn the hair-shirt of secret guilt long enough and the time has come to bare my soul. It is not a pretty sight, I warn you, so if you don't mind I'll keep my vest on.

It can be said in mitigation that I never cheated in school examinations. Our headmaster used to keep a graph of the progress of his less bright pupils, and any upward movement on the steady plateau of my academic achievement would have aroused immediate suspicion. It would have been comparable to an earthquake measuring force nine on the Richter scale, and set alarm bells ringing throughout the school.

No, my cheating began on the sports field rather than in the class-room, when I was forced to enter a cross-country run. Half-way along the route I hopped on a bus

– no one saw me because I was last of the field – and jumped off at a quiet spot not too far from the finish. To lessen the enormity of the deed I kept jogging on the platform. My ruse was never discovered, not that it really mattered anyway, because I came in tenth. But the seeds were sown.

Later in life I was not averse to flicking my golf ball out of the rough on the fairway with the toe of my shoe. This ploy is called 'using the leather mashie'. I gave up cheating at golf after playing a round with Eric Sykes. My ball had disappeared into a thick clump of trees and I found it nestling under some bushes in an unplayable position. I took the only possible way out and threw it out to land quite near the green.

'Splendid shot,' said Sykes as I emerged from the undergrowth.

'Thank you,' I said. 'Miraculous, really.' I dipped my head modestly.

'Especially when you consider the fact that you left all your clubs in your bag on the fairway.'

I looked down and found that I had taken my golf umbrella into the wood with me instead of my wedge. 'It's a shot I read about in *Golf World*,' I said quickly. 'The umbrella wedge shot.'

'Let's see you do it again.' Eric seemed interested.

Sweating slightly, I took a swing at my ball with the umbrella. I missed completely, hitting the ground behind it and causing the handle to fly off.

He said nothing, but the next time his ball went into the rough, he took his own umbrella with him. Sure enough, out came his Dunlop 65 repaint, dead on line for the flag, and finished up only a few inches from the hole.

'Works like a charm,' said Sykes, grinning like an ape through a gap in the leaves. 'Thanks for the tip.'

'Think nothing of it,' I said through clenched teeth. I knew I had met my master.

Cheating

Cheating at sport is a time-honoured custom, although it goes under the name of sportsmanship. Even the great cricketer W. G. Grace was not immune to it. There is a famous story about his coming out to bat in a county match. The first ball clipped the bails and sent one flying.

Unperturbed he turned to the umpire and said, 'Nasty breeze sprung up today.'

'Yes, sir,' replied the umpire. 'Make sure it doesn't blow your cap off on the way back to the pavilion.'

To return to my own guilt-ridden career, I have to reveal that I have cheated in the theatre. When the musical *Pickwick* opened in Manchester prior to its London début, I had great difficulty at the dress rehearsal in remembering the verses of 'If I Ruled the World'. The lyric had to be sung at a fast bolero rhythm and once I made a mistake, the relentless tempo made it impossible to get back on the right track again. And so, with typical lack of courage, I cheated. The sets, by Sean Kenny, were all made of wooden frames and bars which, when manipulated by actor stage managers in the chorus, came together like pieces in a jigsaw puzzle, forming the Fleet Prison one minute, then in the next The George and Vulture, or the election hustings at Eatanswill, the scene in which I sang 'If I Ruled the World' to the company. In front of me, as I sang, was a bar upon which I used to lean as I addressed the crowd. On this bar I decided to write down in a thick felt pen both verses of the song, so that as I looked down benevolently on the company as innocent old Pickwick, the scheming, cheating Secombe could at the same time read the words.

It proved highly successful and every night I would bow my head as far as my bald wig would allow and refer to my crib as I belted out a song advocating honesty and all the old-fashioned virtues. One Monday night, however, things went badly awry. Over the weekend the stage management decided to repaint the scenery and when I got to my appointed position to sing the song, I was faced with a bland bar of wood with not a word of the verses left on it.

'Friends, dear friends,' I began, knowing that much by heart and no more. I don't know exactly what I did sing, I was only aware of a puzzled company staring up at me, and my wig swivelling round on my head as I turned it from side to side in a wild attempt to find the words on the other parts of the woodwork surrounding me.

Afterwards, a friend of mine who was in the audience came backstage and with moist eyes congratulated me on the moving way I had sung the song. And such is the nature of the cheat that I made no attempt to disillusion him by telling the truth.

It was in another musical, *The Four Musketeers*, that I performed my greatest confidence trick on an unsuspecting audience. Before the show opened I had contracted a severe throat infection and to be on the safe side, in case I had a recurrence of it, we made a voice track of the two big numbers in the show. This meant that I could then mime to my own voice while the orchestra in the pit played live. Sure enough, I developed a sore throat one night early in the run, and rather than put my understudy on we used the tape. The theatre manager made an announcement about my having tonsillitis, but that I would be appearing even though it meant using pre-recordings of two main songs.

When the actual time came for me to mime I began well enough, taking it seriously, until my sense of humour got the better of me. I stuffed a handkerchief in my mouth as the tape went on, and the people in the audience realised that I was miming. They began to laugh, and carried away by their amusement, I went into rather a mad ad-lib routine. As the show was not overladen with comedy, through nobody's fault except

Dumas, we decided to keep this in even when my voice got better.

And so for night after night the announcement would be made about my 'throat ailment' and I would go on stage and make a mockery of a lovely song. That was years ago, and people still come up to me and say, 'I was in the audience at Drury Lane that night when you lost your voice.'

There, I feel better now. I think I can take off my hair shirt, so pardon me while I have a good scratch. Ooh, that's lovely.

Fat Chance

I AM PROBABLY the only man for whom a wide has been signalled by the umpire before a ball has even been bowled. I have also been described as a 'heavy roller to be used between innings' by one overly jocular commentator. At one time when I was batting in a charity match with Colin Milburn at Bickley Park, someone claimed that as we ran between the wickets the earth shook for miles in all directions. Such allusions to my weight and size are all meant in fun, and I take no exception to them, but deep down I yearn to spring around the field like Derek Randall, bat with the confidence of Ian Botham and bowl with the dexterity of Derek Underwood. 'Fat chance,' you cry, and well you may. But a man can dream.

Before the start of the first match of the season, in my mind's eye I can see myself striding towards the wicket, bat tucked firmly under my arm, the collar of my crisp white shirt raised up to protect the back of my neck, pads gleaming, boots immaculate, cap slightly tilted at a jaunty angle. I take guard, pat the crease with authority, then take a cool look around at the field placings, smile slightly and prepare to face the first ball. The bowler rushes in, snorting like a bull, and whips his arm over savagely, releasing a bumper at my head. I pick it up immediately with my eye and, moving the feet at just the right moment, I hit the ball hard towards the boundary. The umpire's hands go up for six and the crowd goes wild.

Of course, it's never like that when the moment comes for me to bat in the first charity match in which I have

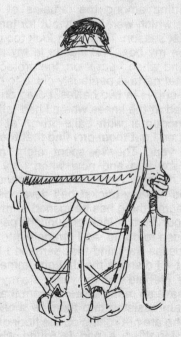

been foolish enough to agree to play. I am usually in the beer tent telling lies about last year's matches when the Captain comes running in to tell us that I'm in next wicket down. That's when the panic starts – its been fun up to now, chatting with the famous cricketers, exchanging banter with the Bedsers, showing Colin Cowdrey how to handle his bat and making other endearing efforts to keep the team happy. Now the jig's up, my bluff is about to be called.

I've only got one pad, I discover when I get back to the dressing-room. 'Where's my box?' I cry, searching frantically in my bag through the debris of last season. I find it nestling among the remains of three cheese sandwiches which were freshly cut for lunch at the last match of last season. They don't look too good now and neither does my box. The elastic in my jock strap has stretched and when I put it on, the protection I need to cover my vital parts is perilously close to disintegration. The plastic cup is in two halves. I drag out my trousers, green-stained at the knees where I had fallen repeatedly to avoid encounter with balls driven at me by Micky Stewart. When I put them on I find that they have shrunk since last year. They've spent eight months doing nothing in my bag and now when I try them on the waistband doesn't meet. What mysterious shrinking propensities has my cricket bag developed during that time? The same thing has happened to my shirt. A light grey in colour from a lack of sunlight perhaps, but the buttons refuse to do up. As I struggle into it the fleeting thought crosses my mind that perhaps I have put on a little weight – I dismiss the thought immediately.

My boots, piebald with the years, are my next problem. The laces have so many knots in them that there is little lace left. I am assisted into them by those members of the team who are not rolling on the floor of the dressing-room with laughter. A pad is found which does not match the one I have, but I am strapped into them, leaving me to face the bowling with what appears to be two left legs. In the battle to dress I find that one half of my support is nestling against my right kneecap. I am about to retrieve it when we hear a great shout from the crowd.

'You're in next. Hurry it up.' The Captain comes in through the door, sees me, and collapses into uncontrollable mirth.

I leave the dressing-room feeling a little hurt as I pull on a pair of batting gloves which have a net total of seven complete fingers and a wedge of cheese sandwich in the thumb.

I wave to the crowd, raising my crumpled Taverners cap with one hand and gesturing regally with the other. When I get half-way to the wicket I realise why I have two hands free to acknowledge the crowd. I have no cricket bat. 'Mr Secombe is going to face the bowling empty-handed. With a figure like his they'll never see his wicket anyway,' says jovial Alan Curtis over the loudspeakers. A bat is produced by a member of the team and I eventually arrive at the crease, heart pounding, a metallic taste in the mouth and my spectacles so steamed up that I can only just make out the opposite wicket. My support is now equally divided between my left knee and my right ankle.

Fred Trueman is called on to bowl to me – regardless of the fact that there are three balls to come from the local bowler. The crowd roars as Fred marks out his run, finishing up on the far boundary. I clutch myself nervously in the area where I feel most bereft. The rest of the side all get behind the wicket, leaving the field to Fred Trueman, the umpire, the other batsman and myself.

'Great sense of humour, has Fred,' says the umpire, chuckling. He begins his run and like a fool I stay at the crease.

He'll drop the ball when he gets to the wicket, I think hopefully. We've had a lot of laughs, old Fred and I. He's still running, and he hasn't dropped the ball yet. The crowd is hysterical. I am hysterical, but not with laughter.

I don't see the ball leave his hand, all I feel is the impact of the ball on my instep. It flies to the boundary and the umpire signals four. I drop the bat and leap around on one foot. The crowd loves it and it takes four team members to carry me back to the pavilion.

That actually happened, and on cold winter's days I can still feel where the ball hit my instep. There's one consolation, though; whenever I get together with cricketers I always say, casually, 'I once made a boundary off Trueman, you know – put him away to leg first ball.'

Tanmanship

BLACK IS BEAUTIFUL, brown is handsome and red is painful. The spectrum of sunburned skins also includes puce, which is the colour I take on when exposed too long to that bright orb in the sky where travel agents go when they die.

No one appreciates the merit of a glorious sun-tan more than I, because I have suffered from the lack of one all my life. I have the kind of skin that goes with a knotted handkerchief and rolled-up trouser legs. No matter what unguents I smooth into it, it crackles and peels. I wouldn't mind that so much if from beneath the first layer of scorched epidermis there emerged a fresh, bronzed Secombe. Unfortunately, under the chrysalid lies just another chrysalid. To make matters worse, I have a wife and four children who go brown within an hour of leaving the aircraft. They develop the jet-set look in the first rays of sunshine while I belong forever to the bi-plane-set. A Sopwith Camel amid a family of Concordes.

Goon Out and About

Not one holiday has gone by without my being laid low with sunburn. There was the time when, after a liquid lunch, I fell asleep in Barbados behind some diamond-shaped trellis work. When I awoke I found that my belly resembled a tudor bow window. On the first day of a vacation in Madeira I lay reading a book in the midday sun wearing a cotton shirt and a pair of Army & Navy shorts, and spent the rest of the ten days in the same position *indoors* with third degree burns on my shins.

Nowadays, having learned my lesson, I always take cricket pads with me when I go abroad. This draws a good deal of attention to myself, but at least I can stand on my own two feet at the end of a long day in the sun and I'm always first choice as wicket-keeper for the beach cricket games.

Fortunes are spent every year by English people in the

effort to acquire the prestige which a tan carries. Plane-loads of holidaymakers take off for the crowded resorts of the Mediterranean with the sole desire to return home done to a cinder so that they can show off to the neighbours. They put up with all sorts of inconveniences for this purpose – unfinished hotel rooms, garlic in everything and the impossibility of ever finding a nice cup of tea. Having arrived at his appointed temple, the true sun worshipper has to go about his task with a grim dedication. He doesn't stand a chance of getting a deckchair or a lilo or a beach umbrella unless he is there on the beach oiled and ready at the crack of dawn. Anytime after seven o'clock the only hope he will have of seeing the sun will be if the lady next to him has pierced ears.

Having chosen a position where he will get the maximum of sun all day, he must also make sure that he gets the benefit of any zephyr that might arise. The best tan always needs a breeze to help it along, so he has to consult the potential wind direction and study sun form like a professional punter before a race. He must expose himself a piece at a time, browning, then re-oiling, turning slowly like a chicken on a spit, basting steadily, following the sun's rays so that they do not fall at too oblique an angle on any part of his body. It is an exhausting, time-consuming process but one which he feels well worthwhile. And when he returns to his office to show off the ebony end product, he finds that he has to apply to the Race Relations Board to get his job back.

I have already mentioned the snob value of a tan and there was no greater evidence of this than when, towards the end of the North African campaign, we of the First Army met up with the famous Eighth Army. We had landed in Algiers in November, 1942, just after the legendary Desert Rats had won the Battle of El Alamein at the other end of the North African coast. For the next six months we fumbled our way eastwards towards Tunis through torrential rain, while the glamorous Eighth dryly swept towards us in the opposite direction.

One day in April our unit exchanged its old sodden battledress for newly sodden tropical kit, and suddenly the sun came out. The steam arising from our drying clothes spread like a cloud across the Tunisian plain as if to hide our modesty from the Germans. Through the mist appeared the first linking elements of the fabulous Eighth with their sand-camouflaged trucks, their Cairo-tailored shorts and desert boots and all of them, every bloody one of them, the colour of mahogany.

We welcomed them awkwardly, our shorts too long, our faces only slightly touched with the sun, and red vees showing at the conjunction of neck and first shirt button. I have never felt so inadequate. They leapt from their vehicles with outstretched hands – a party of Dr. Livingstones greeting a tribe of querulous Stanleys. We were jealous of their reputation and their arrogance, but most of all we envied their tanned skins.

'Get your knees brown!' shouted one desert campaigner to me, looking at the inch and a half of red skin which showed between shorts and stocking tops.

'We've had shocking weather,' I said lamely.

He laughed heartily, and it was only a small consolation when a few minutes later we had a sudden downpour of rain and we had to help to winch their trucks out of the liquid mud, which was as natural an element to us as the sand was to them.

It was a classic example of tanmanship. To have a tan when all around are losing theirs, or have no hope of getting one.

I will leave the last word on the subject with a Jamaican lady we met on holiday some years ago, who kept a little kiosk at the entrance to Doctor's Cave Beach in Montego Bay. She used to sell what is probably the best sun-tan oil of all – pure coconut oil – in Coca Cola bottles with a wedge of paper as a stopper. We got to know her very well (she thought I had married into a West Indian family), and one day as she handed us our bottle and helped to fasten my cricket pads, she looked out at all the motionless bodies sizzling on the sand and observed, 'Man, all dese rich folk coming here, spending all dis money just to get de same colour I was born with. Sure is a funny old world.' And she threw back her head and laughed.

In Praise of Rain

THERE'S A LOT to be said for rain, as Messrs. Macintosh, Burberry and Aquascutum would testify. So would Mr. Galosh – or whoever it was who invented galoshes.

I happen to know the name of the man who invented the umbrella – Jonas Hanway (1712–1786). He was a philanthropist who also travelled extensively abroad, where he took note of people using parasols to keep off the sun. When he returned to London he very sensibly adapted the parasol to protect himself from the rain. Sedan chair carriers, sensing the end of their era, used to pelt him with mud in the streets. The fact that he was a bachelor and carried a handbag may have added strength to their aim. His mortal remains lie in the crypt of St. Mary's Church, Hanwell, of which my brother, Fred, happens to be the Rector.

Fred once had an hilarious experience when conducting a funeral service in a parish in Wales during a heavy downpour. The mourners had assembled around the open grave and he was intoning the bit about 'ashes to ashes' when the sides caved in and he found himself standing on the dear departed's coffin along with the sexton. The resultant scramble to get out developed into a knockabout farce as more people slithered in. Grief turned to laughter and a good time was had by all, proving that rain can have a therapeutic effect, though in this case it was somewhat diminished by my brother's subsequent bronchitis.

I was born during a slight drizzle one September night in Swansea. My home town has always had its fair share of rain – indeed there is a saying that 'if you can see the Mumbles Pier it is about to rain, and if you can't see it, it's already raining'.

I well remember the feeling of relief when rain caused school sports days to be cancelled. The thought of having to leap around making a fool of myself in front of all those people used to make me feel sick – funny how one's attitude changes as one gets older. The athletic lads, smelling of wintergreen and liniment, would jog up and down in the pavilion, calves bursting with frustration as they watched the rain teem down on the lumpy sports field, while old spotty 'four-eyes' Secombe would settle down with secret glee to read his dog-eared D. H. Lawrence.

At another time, later on in my life, rain saved me from going berserk. It was during the war in Italy in 1944 and I had just been posted from a convalescent depot to a Royal Artillery Training Depot prior to being sent back up the line to my unit, a prospect which I did not find particularly appealing. It was near Christmas and I didn't fancy having my stocking filled with a mortar bomb, especially if I happened to be wearing it at the time.

The first night I was there I left my tent – we were all under canvas – and headed for the NAAFI. There was the usual two-fingered pianist banging away on a beer-

stained piano, and after a few half pints of vermouth I
was egged on to do a comic turn by some of the lads
who had been with me at the Convalescent Camp. The
entertainment-starved audience, who were just a shade
drunker than I was, seemed to enjoy my improvisations
and someone suggested that I should audition for the
Camp Concert Party. The chance to spend Christmas in
safety was too good to miss and the following night I
found myself on stage at the camp cinema. All went well
and I was duly enrolled as a semi-permanent member of
the concert party. 'You'll have to move down to the tent
near the cinema. We're pushed for space I'm afraid,' said
the Sergeant in charge.

The tent in question was full of strange paraphernalia
of an unmilitary nature. A wooden lamp-post leaned
against the centre pole, a large painted cabinet
dominated the far end opposite the entrance, and the
place was strewn with packs of cards. As I sat down
heavily on the nearest bed I realised that I had fallen
amongst magicians.

'Excuse me,' said a high-pitched North Country voice.
'You're sitting on my bed of nails.' I got up sharply and
found that I was. The owner of the voice was wearing a
turban low over his eyes, an improvised burnous made
from an Army blanket, and an apologetic expression. He
introduced himself as 'Abdul the Oriental magician', and
asked me to pick a card – any card – from a pack he held
before me. I did so. He shuffled the cards carefully, cut
them three times and held up the four of clubs.

'That's your card,' he said triumphantly.

'No, it's not,' I said, holding up the ten of hearts. 'You
didn't ask me to put it back in the pack.'

'Oh, bloody hell.' He snatched the card back. 'Sorry,'
he said. 'I'm really an illusionist, but me doves flew off
yesterday and I've got to fill in with card tricks.'

He shuffled off, literally, and was replaced by the three

other occupants of the tent. They introduced themselves as 'Mad Max', the comical conjuror, who wore a top hat and white silk scarf with his battledress; 'Mistero', a sleek-headed bombardier with heavy eyebrows, and 'Deirdre', an effeminate Gunner with false eyelashes, who acted as Mistero's assistant in his mind-reading act. I was what they had been waiting for – someone upon whom to try out their tricks. A guinea pig for a bunch of amateur conjurors.

For three weeks I was subjected to their cajolery to 'take a card', or 'guess where the ace of clubs is now'. I was forced to check that Mistero's blindfold was secure while Deirdre minced about the tent holding up different objects for him to identify. 'Your time's up.' 'A watch!' 'Correct.' And my nights were broken by a drunken Abdul mourning for his lost doves.

I even thought of rejoining my unit in action – a sure sign that I was cracking up. Then one night about twelve o'clock the rain came. Gently at first – then a steady drumming on the canvas. A trickle of water began to seep under the bottom of the tent walls. We were pitched on a slope and the water quickly gathered momentum as the rain got heavier. We were playing cards – what else? – by the light of an oil lamp when Mistero, whose two-inch brow was furrowed with the effort of trying to read my hand, looked down and noticed that his ankles were awash. Within minutes the whole tent was flooded, and to my intense delight I found myself surrounded by floating playing cards. I opened the tent flap and watched them float away. Something nudged the back of my legs. It was the bed of nails. I stood aside and let it disappear into the night. Behind me there were cries of anguish from the coven of conjurors as they strove to rescue their props.

'Me frock's ruined!' cried Deirdre.

'That's show business,' I said, splashing him playfully

with water from Max's top hat. Then the tent collapsed.

In concluding my case in praise of rain I must tell of the most rewarding experience of my theatrical life. I was playing Kalgoorlie, the famous gold-mining town in Western Australia, during a period of prolonged drought. The venue was a football field on the outskirts of the town, and the stage was an improvised one. The night was warm and the sky was cloudless when I began my performance. By the time I had reached 'Bless This House', thunder had started over the east. 'Bless these walls so firm and stout' I sang nervously as the flimsy canvas screen behind me flapped wildly in the sudden breeze. When I got to the bit about dwelling 'Oh Lord with Thee', lightning flickered over the field and I thought He was about to exact just retribution for ten thousand wrong notes. Then down came the rain – the unexpected, long-awaited rain – and to a man the audience got to its feet and gave me the biggest ovation I have ever had.

I felt as Harold Wilson must have done when standing outside No. 10 Downing Street one sunny morning. A passer-by called to him, 'Lovely day, sir.' The then Prime Minister gave a slight bow. 'Thank you,' he said.

Fat is Beautiful

THERE IS A conspiracy (and I use the word advisedly – I also use the word contumely, but there isn't much demand for it these days) against fat people in this country. It is my considered opinion that Britain, having shed most of its class distinction, is now divided in a different way: those who are fat and those who are thin. Lean people are the new aristocracy and we fat ones are the plebs.

According to the trendy magazines and those who peddle advice to readers in the columns of the popular press, it's a sin to be overweight. We are bombarded with diets of all descriptions. Ladies like greyhounds stand smiling proudly alongside cardboard cut-outs of their previous shapes, while those of us who retain our surplus weight are supposed to creep about shame-facedly wearing sackcloth and ashes. Sackcloth, incidentally, is all a large person can find to wear in these skeletal times. All the smart clothes are designed

51

for the slimmer figure, and portly people have to put up with more dowdy apparel. 'Slim yourself into new clothes,' they say. Diet and you have to throw away your old suits. It's a confidence trick perpetrated by the tailoring profession and health food shop proprietors. 'Lose weight and live longer,' they exhort us. Yet I can think of nothing more tragic than dieting for a three-month period, enduring all the misery which that entails, and then, on the day after one has finished, stepping off the kerb with a new-found sprightliness right into the path of a bus.

Insurance tables conspire against us. Those plaques giving average weights for height and age on weighing machines are also a deliberate policy of harassment against fat people. I should be ten foot tall and 105 years of age.

Another area where overweight folk are taken to task by the media is in the field of romance. One has only to read the agony columns of women's magazines to get the picture. 'My boyfriend says I'm too fat and has threatened to leave me,' laments 'Worried of Walthamstow', who, let us assume for our argument, is a lady. 'You must slim to keep him, dear,' is the stern reply. Why in heaven's name should she? If he is anything like the average Romeo he will be too busy admiring his skinny profile in the mirror to notice whether she's lost weight or not. She will be far better off with someone of her own ilk who would appreciate her cuddly proportions. I might even drop her a line myself.

There was a time, I admit, when I tried every kind of advertised diet – milk diets, banana diets, even mashed potato diets. Some of them worked for a while and I became a diet bore. 'Look,' I would say to anyone I could force into a corner, 'I've lost weight.' Then I would tug at the waistband of my trousers and show how my belly was disappearing. I would extoll the virtues of ridding oneself of surplus fat at every available opportunity, demonstrating even as I spoke how the firm, fat chins I had once possessed now hung like wattles on a Norfolk turkey. And all the time underneath I was unhappy, because I began to realise that I have a naturally fat nature, and I am also a fat thinker.

I don't know why there should be this prejudice against being overweight. Fat spells comfort, placidity, peace of mind. My mother was fat and when I was a child and in distress I used to hurl myself into her billowing bosom for solace. If a modern child were to hurl himself into his mother's arms today he would be liable to get severely bruised. I love words like fat, jumbo, plump, butter, lard, balloon, chubby. They have a jolly ring about them. Whereas lean, gaunt, thin, angular, bony and skinny all have a sinister sound. 'Let me have men about me that are fat; . . . Yond Cassius has a lean and hungry look; He thinks too much: such men are dangerous,' said Shakespeare's Julius Caesar.

I have a theory that most of our present troubles are caused by people who are thin or who are trying to lose weight. The restless business tycoon pacing the plush carpet in his penthouse office suite with its panoramic views of the city, fresh and snarling from two weeks in a health farm, could wreak financial havoc on the stock exchange; forcing me to the conclusion that people in glass houses shouldn't cast stones. Urban guerillas and other terrorists whose pictures fill our news media are all lean, hungry-looking men. I have yet to see fat thugs darting across roads with machine guns or leaping over the barriers at football matches. Apart from the obvious physical limitations involved in these pursuits, it's not in our nature to indulge in them. We would rather eat than fight. Hitler was much thinner than Churchill – and we all know who started that fight. I am sure that our great war-time leader would have preferred to sit in his armchair by the fire with a large brandy than clobber the Germans, and it's certain that the Nazis were sorry that he ever heaved himself out of it. Unfortunately, after the war we heaved him out of office in favour of thin Clement Attlee along with the equally thin Stafford Cripps, and we lost the Empire.

One day, if things go wrong and some lean fanatic in Washington or Moscow or Peking presses that dreadful button, all the thin people in the world will look at each other in the realisation of what they have wrought, and in the last remaining seconds they will rush for comfort to the few fat folk who are left. And we will rock them in our arms and pat their backs and say 'There, there.' Because that's what fat people are for.

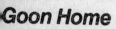
Goon Home

Calling Dream Control

WHEN I WAS a boy I shared a bed with my older brother. In such close proximity one tends to find out quite a lot about one's companion's nocturnal habits and eccentricities. My brother had one particular gift which I envied: an ability to regurgitate his supper. He would lie there in our communal kip contentedly munching away at the fish and chips which he had consumed half an hour previously. Every time I tried to do the same the consequences were dire in the extreme. However, there was one thing which I was able to do and he was not. This was a knack of deciding what I would dream about beforehand and, composing myself for sleep, I would drift into my chosen fantasy at will.

It must be said that at that time I was a great Tarzan fan. Therefore, it was pretty easy for me to drum up a dream about him, and he figured largely in my predetermined nightly adventures. Later came the mattress-thrashing of puberty, when Jane featured rather more prominently. It was a feat of my conscious mind over the subconscious, which I have allowed to lapse over the years, having had other things to occupy my thoughts – World War II, four children and the prospect of an Irish atom bomb being some of them.

Recently, though, there came into my possession a cutting from an American newspaper which quotes an Assistant Professor called Tom Bond. 'You don't have to be a victim of your dreams,' he says. 'With a little practice you can learn to control your dreams by following a few easy steps.' He goes on to list them. 'First, you have to believe dreams are important. Next, find a nice spot and decide what you are going to dream. Then make up a catch-phrase about the subject and repeat it to yourself during the day.' (Bond likes to dream about flying, so his phrase is 'Tonight I fly' or, possibly, 'Flying tonight'.) 'Finally, about ten minutes before retiring, pick a quiet spot and really concentrate on what you want to dream about.'

I instantly resolved to find out whether I still retained the old cunning. I decided that as a trial run it might be a good idea to choose Tarzan as my subject for dream control, having had such success with him in my youth.

In the interests of science, here are my notes from Tuesday night to Wednesday morning . . .

All day have been saying 'Tonight I am Tarzan'. Get home from theatre. Find note, left by wife. 'Me Jane – got migraine. Asleep in spare room.' Preparations for bed. Make drink of hot milk. Lie back on pillow and concentrate on Tarzan. Start wondering whether any leopard-skin big enough to fit me. Better ask Dream Control to check with Wardrobe. Dismiss thought as irrelevant. Think of Johnny Weismuller riding an elephant. Word association. Become aware of fly buzzing around the room. Thought they were all dead by this time of year. Try to ignore it. Lands on forehead, walks sluggishly down nose. Put light on. Fly takes off slowly from pillow. Hit it with *Evening Standard*. Easy kill. Put light off. *'Tonight I am Tarzan.'* Settle back again.

Late-night bus stops outside. Live on main road. Bus stop opposite. Conductor shouts 'Harry's Corner.' People in double deckers often see me in my vest at bedroom window. Wave to me – wave back. Engine throbs away, voices raised – unable to understand what is being said. Put light on. Go to window and part curtains. 'If I ruled the world' sings a drunken voice up to window. Hurriedly back away. Song continues through three changes of key up the street, becomes duet, finishes in distance in argument over words.

'Tonight I am Tarzan,' I say through gritted teeth. Do dissolve into jungle. Waterfall running over giant boulders. Think of Victoria Falls. Think of Niagara Falls. Think of Falls Road, Belfast. Turn over on stomach trying to forget full bladder. Reluctantly leave bed for toilet along landing. Pass spare bedroom door.

'That you, Harry?'

'Yes.'

'Did you put the gas off?'

'Of course.'

Back in bed again. *'Tonight I am Tarzan.'* Did I put the gas off? Can't remember. Must have done. Fancy I can smell gas. New stove – not accustomed to controls – might have left milk saucepan on low light. Go back downstairs. Forget burglar alarm switched on. Open kitchen door. Alarm goes off. Switch if off. Wife half-way downstairs.

'Just checking stove.'

Back in bed. Breathing heavily. Heart pounding with exertion of climbing stairs. Just the right age for heart attack. Overweight. Think thin. Tomorrow I diet. *'Tomorrow I diet.'* No, that's not the one. *'Tonight I am Tarzan.'* Put hand on chest. Heart beat feels erratic.

Swallow air and bring up wind. That's better – must be indigestion. Can't go swinging through the jungle with heartburn. Get up and go to bathroom for Alka Seltzer.

'Is that you, Harry?'

Confirm it is I with loud belch.

'Charming,' says wife. 'You shouldn't have such long lunches, then you wouldn't have to stay up all night writing.'

'Not writing. Doing research for article.'

'Same thing.'

Can't think of reply. Go back to bed. Think of reply, then think better of it.

Tonight I am Tarzan.' Feel myself falling, falling into dense undergrowth . . .

'Cup of tea.'

I grope bleary-eyed for the proffered mug with Taurus on it. Virgo one got broken.

'How's Tarzan this morning?'

'Who?'

'Tonight I am Tarzan,' my wife reminds me, beating her chest and yodelling. 'Did it work?'

All I can remember is a jumbled dream of being aboard a bus with Alka Seltzer tablets for wheels and driven by a large fly. Upstairs a hundred drunken Pickwicks sang 'If I ruled the world'. Downstairs there was only me, but I filled the bus. I was an elephant.

'Not really,' I say, sipping my tea.

Why, If It Isn't Old What'sit . . .

ONE SUNDAY AFTERNOON some years ago I was dancing to the music behind the BBC-2 Test Card with my four-year-old daughter when the front door bell rang. My wife and the rest of my progeny were scattered around the house deep in post-prandial naps, so I bravely ventured to the door wearing my usual Sunday outfit of vest, trousers and bare feet. My wife had told me that the milkman would be calling and that she had left the money on the sideboard for him. I opened the door yelling 'Milko!' into the faces of an immaculately-dressed middle-aged couple.

'You're not the milkman,' I said.

'No, indeed,' they chorused, looking at me as if they expected me to know them.

'You won't want the money then,' I said foolishly, putting the cash in the trouser pocket with the hole in it.

They stood patiently, unmoving, as I retrieved the coins from the doorstep. 'Well, we decided to accept your kind offer and drop in when we were passing. We were on our way from Birmingham to Ilford, so here we are.'

Working out the distance quickly I realised that they had made a detour of about twenty miles. We live in Cheam. I supposed I should have known them but their faces meant nothing to me.

'I see,' I said cleverly, suddenly aware that I hadn't shaved that morning.

'Yes,' they said, nodding and smiling.

This pantomime went on for some time until the arrival of my small daughter, Katy, who pointed at the woman and said, 'That's the lady with the very close legs.'

'Varicose,' I said, unthinking.

Then it suddenly hit me. This was the couple we had met briefly in Barbados. They had a cottage next-door-but-one to us for a week and we had only ever seen them in bathing costumes, sunglasses and covered in sun tan lotion. We used to nod to them when we passed each other on the beach and their only distinguishing features were her varicose veins and his blistered bald head. We knew them as the Bonce and the Road Map.

'Very close for the time of year,' I said hurriedly, seeing the woman's face suffuse. 'Come on in. You will have to take us as you find us.'

They followed me into the lounge, wading ankle deep through Sunday newspapers on the way. One of our boxer dogs came in and knocked the man over. The noise woke Myra, my wife, who came downstairs in her old dressing-gown demanding to know what was going on. By this time I had rescued the man from the dog and was sticking things under cushions to make the place look a bit tidy.

'This is . . . um, you know, from Barbados.'

My wife remembered. 'Of course,' she said, 'Tom and Doris. You invited them to drop in and see us any time. It was the night of the party when you were ill after the rum punches.'

Tom and Doris sat down on the settee, mollified, stayed until twelve o'clock that evening and ate us out of house and home. I drove them to the station, and on the way back I had a puncture.

'Serves you right,' said Myra, not too unkindly. 'You should never make promises when you have had a few drinks – especially on holiday.'

She was right, of course, but there's something about being on holiday abroad that makes one seek out one's fellow man. Friendships spring up more easily when one is away from one's own restricting environment. In some cases holidaymakers strike up lasting relationships on the journey out. I remember one such trip a few years ago when I was flying out with my elder daughter, Jennifer, to Majorca. It had been a pretty exhausting day for me one way and another, and the plane's delay had provided the opportunity for rather more solace at the bar in the airport lounge than was good for me. I sat near the window next to Jennifer, whose neighbour on her other side was a rather garrulous lady. Soon after take-off I fell asleep. The next thing I knew was that I was being prodded in the stomach by the fat woman.

'It is, isn't it?' she cried, grabbing my hand. 'You are that man on the telly – Harry Secombe – aren't you? I thought I recognised you. You've made my holiday.' She leaned back again in her seat. 'That's the second time I have been lucky,' she commented to my daughter. 'Last year I went to Rome and I saw the Pope.'

I still get letters from her and so, I presume, does the Pope.

Some holiday relationships last longer than others. The flotsam of the tide of past summers is usually washed up on the mantelpiece each year in the form of Christmas cards. 'Happy Days – Cynthia and Horace'; 'Remember that summer at Positano – love, Jack and Mabel' say the cards, causing faint bells to ring in the back of one's mind. Have we sent them one? Have they moved? Didn't she say that Tom had died last year? Are they still together? People you meet on holiday can send you to a psychiatrist.

Whereas the chance companions one meets on some foreign strand can become life-long friends, I have also found that to go on holiday with friends can be disastrous. Myra and I once made the mistake of taking a short weekend in Paris with a couple with whom we had been friendly for years – let's call them Lillian and Jim Brown. They were a handsome couple and I had always secretly envied Jim's debonair manner and his quiet elegance. Myra admired Lillian for her wit and sharp intellect. I don't think they felt the same way about us.

The trip started off quite merrily with drinks on the

plane, and Jim soon had the hostesses laughing at his innuendoes.

'Lover boy's at it again,' said Lillian a little sharply, downing her third champagne cocktail.

'Don't get too sloshed, darling.' Jim's voice carried an edge.

By the time we arrived at the hotel they weren't speaking to each other. At dinner, Jim pointedly ignored Lillian, who had quite a load on by this time and was taunting him openly.

'Ask him to tell you about the time when his secretary's husband punched him on the nose,' she demanded of me, stabbing my elbow with her fork.

'There's a good show on at the Lido,' said Myra brightly.

'She'll be too sozzled to appreciate it.' Jim pinched the bottom of a passing waitress as he spoke.

She turned and clipped me across the earhole.

'Hooray!' shrieked Lillian, clapping her hands with delight.

'It wasn't me, it was him.'

Myra looked at me strangely. While I was convincing her that I was telling the truth, Jim and Lillian got up and left the restaurant arguing loudly. I was burdened with the bill and an aching earhole.

We didn't see them again until we set out for the airport the following morning. They seemed quite happy together for a change, though conversation was desultory on our part. They started rowing again when we found out that fog had closed Heathrow Airport and that the only way home was by train and ferry. The journey was a nightmare of long hours standing in the train corridor listening to Jim and Lillian exchanging pleasantries. When we arrived at Calais there was a porters' strike and we had to carry our own luggage. On the way through customs a short man wearing a large velvet trilby offered to help me with one of my cases.

'Thank you, Sir George,' I said gratefully, using my then current form of address to strangers.

'Sir John,' he said, picking up the case, 'Sir John Barbirolli.'

'Really?' I said, dropping the rest of my luggage and seeking his hand. 'You know, you've made my holiday.'

And he had.

Just Jim

IT'S OUR JIM'S tenth birthday today – as near as we can
tell, anyway – so my wife is baking a special cake which
he will eat all by himself, starting with the candles. He is
going grey and his eyes are getting rheumy and he's a bit
stiff in the mornings, but for a ten-year-old boxer he's
doing fine. There's only one thing wrong with him: he
thinks he's a person, and nothing we do can convince
him otherwise. I've even caught him secretly practising
walking on his hind legs. He had the grace to look
sheepish when he saw me watching, but he had nerve
enough to keep on trying.

I bought him as a companion for my wife and children
when I was on tour and they were alone in the house.
Myra – my wife – said, 'Get a big one while you're at it.
There's no good getting a lap dog, you haven't got a lap.'

Smarting under the sarcasm, I went to some kennels
near where I was playing in pantomime and asked to see
some boxer puppies. I was shown around the kennels

but couldn't make up my mind which one to have until we went into the farmhouse for a cup of tea, and there was this clown of a puppy snoozing near the fire surrounded by kittens.

'That's the one for me,' I said. 'Unconventional – obviously a character. What's his name?'

'Jim – just Jim,' said the lady, picking him up and handing him to me. He yawned sleepily and drew blood from my nose with his sharp little teeth. I had to buy him then, if only to get my own back when he got a bit older.

When I got him home he was immediately spoiled by the family, a situation in which he revelled until he disgraced himself here and there.

However, as he got older his character began to assert itself. He had, and still has, a confused sense of loyalties. The back door he will protect against all comers, including us, but anybody can come in through the front door. This has earned him the title 'The Burglar's Friend'.

To this day, if ever we want to move his great hulk from in front of the fire we only have to say 'Cats' and off he goes to the top of the garden and barks his head off at nothing. You can do this any time, and he never seems to catch on, though after doing it three times in succession one cold winter's night, his bark the third time did not seem to carry much conviction, and when he trotted back in he gave me a hard look before slumping under the table.

When he reached twelve months, I decided it might be a good thing for all concerned if I sent him away to be trained. He kept jumping up at people and licking them all over as they lay prostrate between his paws. This boisterous way of saying 'Hello' was costing us friends, so I took him along to a place where they sort out canine eccentrics.

As I left, a kennel boy in a white coat was being

dragged off his feet by Jim as he went for a startled retriever. They'll soon cure him of that, I thought. When he gets home he'll be using a knife and fork.

We rang, as we were told to do, on the first Sunday.

'He's quite a character, your Jimmy,' said a voice. 'We haven't been able to put him with the other dogs yet, but he's settling down.'

The following week we were informed that he was still on his own, and that he had killed a chicken. Four days later we were asked to remove him as he was a bad influence on the other dogs.

I drove out to collect him, expecting to find the place besieged by Jim leading a pack of savage dogs. It wasn't as bad as that, though. When the kennel boy brought him out he was pulled flat on his face by Jim's sudden joyous burst of speed on seeing me. Sighing, I opened the door, let Jim in and drove away with one hand, fighting off a deliriously slobbering boxer with the other.

That was the end of his education. Strangely enough, some of the commands he learned linger in a shadowy corner of his brain, and if by chance I say in sheer exasperation 'Lie down', he might do just that. But he won't get up until the next command unlocks his reflexes. 'Up!' No. 'Get up!' No. He looks silly lying there in the middle of the road waiting for the password. 'Here boy'; that's the one. He gets to his feet and saunters on, exhausted with his mental effort. He's a canine Eccles.

Two years ago the vet said that he had a rare kidney complaint and had not long to live. This was terrible, and to soften the blow of his passing I went and bought another boxer puppy for the children – a bitch.

At first we thought he would eat her. Having been master of the household for so long he resented intrusion, and he nearly went mad with rage. It didn't take him long to find out that she was a lady though, and a new look came into his eye. We could see him lying under the table working it all out and beginning to like the idea.

Cindy, the newcomer, was a born coquette and soon had him eating out of her paw. He looked a big stupid oaf, lolloping around the garden after her, his jowls drooling in fervent anticipation. There was no sign of the old Jim; his coat was shining, his nose was wet, and in six months he was the father of half a dozen puppies.

The children insisted on keeping one of them, and like fools we agreed. Now we have three boxers: a heavyweight, a welterweight and a featherweight. I've been working it out – if we carry on this way in five years' time we shall be knee-deep in boxers.

For what it's worth I have a theory that the dogs are slowly taking over the country – they couldn't make a worse mess of it than we have done. That's why we baked a cake for Jim's birthday: he might be Prime Minister one day. He's got the face for it.

Goon Overseas

Majorca

I

THERE IS A pleasure boat which leaves Cala Bona for Cala Ratjada twice a day during the season, and as it nears a peninsula called Costa de los Pinos, a guide with a megaphone points out the various luxurious houses. 'This is da house of Jackie Kennedy. Over there is da villa from Franco. Dat one wid da red roof is belong to King Juan Carlos. And dis one wid da big pool and da white tower is da villa of 'Arry Secombes. All together, English peoples, shout "'Ello 'Arry".'

The passengers, loaded to the gunwales with fiery alcoholic concoctions which they will subsequently lose over the side on the way back, raucously obey. Right on cue a short, stout man appears on his patio and waves a hand in greeting. The passengers wave back and the flamenco-damaged vessel ploughs on.

Now, I have a confession to make. That villa is not mine – I should be so lucky – and the short, stout chap is an extremely wealthy Spanish businessman who is awakened every day from his siesta by this unaccountable shouting, and he is not waving, he is shaking his fist. Meanwhile, tucked away in the pines, I lie back on my rickety bamboo lounging chair and chuckle quietly to myself.

I am sorry to destroy this illusion of the glamorous film-star life that British visitors to Majorca seem to think I lead, but at least I am able to preserve a certain amount of privacy in my own modest holiday home. After all, that is why I bought the place – for privacy. I am quite prepared to endure the good-natured banter of my fellow passengers on the flight out – 'Sing us a song, 'Arry boy,' they cry; ''Ere, aint he gorn grey!'; 'Aren't you different in the flesh?' One large lady once held me firmly by the arm in the airport lounge, looked long and hard into my face, and then called back to her travelling companions, 'No, it's not him.' But when I arrive in Majorca I like to merge quietly into the background – a task comparable with that of Ian Paisley seeking an audience with the Pope. However, I do try, and it's easier out of season when the tourists are thin on the ground and only the spartan Germans stride bare-legged through the rain-swept lanes.

That is the time when the British residents come out from their summer hibernation, hurriedly check the position of the pound against the peseta in the *Majorca Daily Bulletin,* take the old blazers out of the mothballs and head for their favourite haunts. Invitations to 'drinks before dinner' drop into letter boxes and over the next few months permutations of the same faces appear in permutations of the same houses. Fortunately, unlike English suburbia, there is no class distinction in these get-togethers. We cling to each other because our 'foreignness' sets us aside from the locals, who regard us with a good-natured intolerance.

For example, if you had been in the main street of Cala

Millor a few years ago you would have witnessed a strange ceremony. A motley collection of British, German and Spanish gathered outside a brand new bar on the corner opposite the Banco de Credito Balear. A short, fat Welshman stood before the closed door, reading a speech. 'This is a corner of a foreign field which is forever Mayorkshire,' I declaimed, expecting a laugh and getting one. A stray dog had cocked its leg against my cream trousers. I cut short the proceedings. 'I hereby declare Andy's Fish and Chip Bar open and God bless all who sail in her.' I kicked the dog surreptitiously and opened the door with a flourish. Champagne flowed freely and Andy and Kathy, two lovely people from Bridlington, were launched into the battle against the domination of the paella.

Out of season is also the time for trying out new restaurants, and once we took a chance on a café run by a German. I began talking to the proprietor in a friendly manner about my army experiences and discovered, a table away, an ex-German soldier with whom I had exchanged shots in North Africa during the war. When I say 'exchanged shots', I mean that the regiment of Artillery of which I was a small part, had presumably fired upon his regiment, of which he was a larger part – being a Feldwebel as opposed to my rank of Lance Bombardier. We had, however, won the battle in question because Hans had finished up in a prisoner-of-war camp in Canada. He said that our unit had actually taken him prisoner. My remorse bought him drink after drink until my wife led me away from the battlefield under a flag of truce.

The next night I went along to the same bar to meet my new-found friend, equipped with maps and books of the North African campaign. I discovered him in deep conversation with an English holidaymaker against whom he had apparently fought in the Battle of Arnhem.

It was only after I had bought the third round of drinks that I realised that if Hans had been captured in 1942 he could not possibly have been at Arnhem in 1944. There was nothing else to do but join in the battle myself. Apparently, before my wife rescued me, I was holding the north end of the Bridge single-handed, armed only with a pocket knife. Old soldiers never die—their livers fade away.

I am ashamed to admit that after fifteen years of owning a holiday home in Majorca I still have difficulty ordering goods in Spanish. This causes much amusement in the village shops. A visit from El Gordo, or the Fat One, as I am known locally, is the nearest thing to entertainment that Son Servera can offer. At the butcher's, a slap on the leg accompanied by 'baa-aa' means leg of lamb, a gesture towards the small of the back and a 'moo' does service for steak, although on one occasion I had a cold and got sweetbreads instead. I daren't ask for sausages.

In spite of the language barrier, my family and I are beginning to understand the working of the Majorcan mind. If you expect promptness from tradesmen, you're in for a big surprise. Shopkeepers will say yes out of politeness. We have had half an iron gate for four years and our shutters are still held back with string. Every six months the local blacksmith calls in for a sherry and looks at the jobs he has left unfinished. He nods, promises, asks after the family, then we ask after his, and that's it for another six months.

We had a hole in the ground for two years waiting to undergo its metamorphosis into a swimming pool. Strange-looking weeds grew out of it, the kids kept falling into it, and every time we came out for a holiday we went through the ritual of pleas, and promises, with the builder. Then suddenly we arrived for an Easter break and it was practically finished. It stayed practically finished until we came back in August. Then there was a flurry of workmen and hey presto, it was completed – all except for the ladder, which was essential to aid my getting in and out without scraping acres of skin off my belly. So I had to sit high and dry like a stranded whale as the rest of the family frolicked in the sparkling water. Then one evening the ladder arrived, unannounced, from Palma. The following morning the water in the pool had almost drained away owing to the loosening of several tiles. I now had a ladder and a pool, but no water. We managed to get all three elements together on the day we had to leave for home. I had a hasty dip and developed an eye infection from an overdose of chlorine.

Yet all these little trials are well worth enduring for the privilege of living part-time in Majorca. Beyond the concrete canyons of Can Pastilla, Arenal and Magaluf there are banks where the wild garlic grows, where honeysuckle blazes in roadside hedges and where you can still hear sheep bells and cocks crowing and the lowing of cattle; where you can buy bread hot from the baker's oven and find little village bars where for twenty-five pesetas you can buy a glass of locally-made liqueur which will blow your brain straight through the top of your sunburned skull. And if you think I am going to tell you where to find them, you must be crazy.

II

'Pedro – it is the fat Englishman,' shouts Antonia in the direction of the bead curtains at the back of the electrician's shop, forgetting that I know enough Majorcan to understand my own nickname in the village. I take my shopping list from my pocket and stand at the counter. She smiles at me and goes back to her perfunctory cleaning of the fridge which has been on special offer for six months. The shop is full of TV sets, fridges, light fittings and pressure cookers, and now me, because it is not a very big place to start with. I turn to examine a pile of cassettes by Spanish pop artists on the counter and knock over a butane gas cylinder. Bending down to pick it up I demolish a set of Pyrex dishes. Antonia rushes to my side, her false teeth clacking like castanets in consternation, and begins to put the shop back in order. I stammer apologies in Italian – for some reason I have a mental blank about speaking Spanish and though I am capable of picking my way through the Spanish newspapers and interpreting the disasters on the TV, my standard of conversation is on the 'Me Tarzan, You Jane' level.

In the midst of the hubbub Pedro, her husband, entered. He was, as usual, unshaven, his stained green pullover unchanged since the onset of winter. A firm believer in not casting a clout till May be out, he retains the same clouts. June will find him in a stained grey pullover. He is an amateur poet, an amateur philosopher and my good friend.

'Olà, Señor,' he says, inadvertently crunching a cassette as he comes through the bead curtains. Antonia lets out a small strangled cry of despair and leaves the shop. With a shrug Pedro kicks the remains of the cassette under an adjacent gas stove and leans on the counter ready for a chat. With the aid of my pocket dictionary and a lot of mime I manage to explain that I have come for the butane heater I left with him to repair last April. It is now February and my wife and I are here for a couple of weeks and the house is cold – 'Frío, muy frío.' I flap my arms across my chest. He nods and brings out a bottle of brandy from under the counter. We drink and he promises to try to come along to the house this afternoon with the heater, although he thinks he may have sold it by mistake. We have another couple of drinks and I buy a brand-new heater which he will definitely install some time today, along with the new toaster I seem also to have bought.

I leave the shop and take a left turn into the little street leading to the main square in Son Servera. Consulting my shopping list I see we need a fresh loaf and two ensaimadas. In the warmth of the baker's the brandy starts to work and I finish up with two loaves hot from the oven and one ensaimada. This is a delicacy found only in Majorca and is a strip of flaky pastry wound around in a flat circle and covered with a dusting of white sugar.

Having parked the car in the square perilously close to the traffic policeman's feet, I make my way carefully to Juan the butcher's. There is a queue of ladies all in black which I join. Some I know by sight and I nod to them, eliciting a smile here, a distant inclination of the head there. Conversation stops momentarily, noses are wrinkled at the smell of brandy at ten-thirty in the morning, and then it begins anew as they discuss me. I look up at the loops of bright red sausages which hang over the counter along with stalactites of thick sobrasadas – a local sausage flavoured with red pepper, which stains the cheeks of the children vivid orange. The queue moves slowly. The women buy portions of chickens rather than whole ones and expect legs and heads to be included. Small gobbets of meat I don't recognise are weighed carefully and taken home for Majorcan dishes which will be delicious when prepared, I'm sure. Juan, the butcher, sees me and in his halting English invites me to come forward to the head of the queue. I take one look at the faces around me and decide to wait my turn. There is talk of witchcraft in Son Servera and I'm not taking chances on sudden stabbing pains in the night.

Back to the car at last, leaving behind a faint ripple of laughter from the customers. I check my list again.

'Carrots, cabbage, onions, garlic,' in my wife's handwriting: '1 bottle of Marques de Riscal and 1 bottle of Fundador' in my own heavier hand. I can get all these in one shop, Miguel's in Cala Bona, which is only a kilometre or two away. The shop is empty and after I've picked the fresh vegetables from the boxes on the floor Miguel invites me to sample a new cask of red wine he has just had delivered. I sip from the glass he offers me with an air of great concentration concealing my utter ignorance of the subject of wine. If it's wet I'll drink it. 'I'll take it as red,' I say cleverly in English. It doesn't translate very well into Spanish. He pours me a glass of a local liqueur. This time I am unable to comment in any language. It takes two more glasses for me to get my breath back. I nod numbly and stagger out of the shop with a bottle of 'Yerbas' with which I shall start the fire.

Miguel helps me to load the car and I drive home through fields full of almond trees in full blossom, though it might be more appropriate to use the road. The air is like wine and the sea a cobalt blue. Outside our house the dingy white of Pedro's van contrasts with the colourful hibiscus and from the chimney comes a wisp of smoke. I get out of the car and heave a sigh of content – who could ask for anything better than Majorca on a lovely February morning?

I open the door of our idyllic holiday home to find my wife putting Pedro out. What I mean is that he has set his pullover on fire testing the new butane heater. There's no real harm done and he gets one of my pullovers to wear. From the way he is feeling the material, Spring is going to be a little late this year.

III

I lay on my back on the only serviceable lounging chair, watching the blue Mediterranean sparkle in the space between the ruined columns of my outstretched legs. A distant fishing boat appeared from behind the enlarged joint of my left big toe and sailed slowly towards the spread toes of my right foot, briefly reappearing four times until it disappeared behind the peninsula of the Pernod bottle. The putt-putting of its engine floated lazily across the water to mingle with the tinkle of the sub- siding ice cubes in the drink at my side, and the gentle popping of the capillaries in my nose.

Around me the patio baked in the noonday sun and even the flies sought the shade. I tilted my straw sombrero over my eyes and raised the glass to my lips. A small fly was cooling its feet on a piece of ice near the surface. Feeling tolerant, I extended a finger and offered it a lift on to dry land. It accepted my assistance reluctantly, drying its wings and legs in a desultory fashion whilst standing on my stomach. Eventually it trudged doggedly over my immediate horizon – a Chris Bonington of the insect world scaling the Everest of my belly. When it reached the downward slope leading to my navel it bit me.

My slapping hand missed it by a mile, and with a final derisory buzz it flew off to join its mates in the shade. Anyway, it will give them something to talk about, I thought. I licked my finger and applied the spittle to the sting. What's an insect bite on a lovely day like this. My wife was out shopping for the afternoon and the house was mine. Majorca out of season is peaceful and calm, I mused drowsily.

'Olà!' said a voice behind me. The electrician had arrived from the village to put up a light fitting we had brought out from England. 'Mucha calor,' said Pedro, squatting on the step and fanning himself with his hat. 'Cchott.' He was wearing his perennial woollen cardigan.

I made a drinking sign with my hand. 'Cerveza?' I enquired.

He shook his head. This was an old game with us. He would refuse two offers and accept gracefully the third. After that there was no stopping him. I brought him a bottle of beer from the fridge.

'Salud!' He sipped appreciatively, smacking his lips. 'Alemán,' he said, looking at the label on the bottle.

'Si,' I said, choosing the word carefully.

He took another long swig from his bottle of German beer and rummaged in his tool box. The search proved fruitless. 'No cchammer. Momento.' He went into the garden.

Two minutes later he returned with a large stone. He held it up. 'Cchammer,' he said. 'Pedro primitivo.' Picking up the bottle, he drained it and belched. 'Bueno,' he said, meaningly, tapping the label with his finger.

I pretended to ignore the message. He sat down again and sighed heavily. 'Too much cchott.'

It was my turn to sigh. 'All right.' I heaved myself from my chair again and brought him another beer.

He took it back into the house with him. I settled back to enjoy the sunshine. I was nodding off nicely when Pedro tapped me on the shoulder. In his hand he held the light fitting.

'Complicado,' he said, waving bits of wire in my face. 'Usted' – he dug me in the chest with his screwdriver – 'Venga con migo.'

I went with him.

'Sistema Inglesa,' he explained. The light dangled from its appointed place on the wall, wires spewing from it. He began a series of elimination on the various wires and when he had considered himself satisfied he asked me to hold the lamp while he switched on the electricity. The shock hurled me across the room.

'No es bueno,' he said, sucking his teeth reflectively. He took the lamp from me and studied it. I lay panting against the wall.

The door opened and five Dutch people came in – two adults and three large flaxen-haired children with whom my eight-year-old daughter had made friends the previous summer. They laughed heartily at my appearance. Everything I did when we met previously they had thought funny, even though we could only communicate in sign language. I got up, trembling, from the floor and tried to convey what had happened. They laughed louder. Pedro joined in, making a huge arc with his screwdriver as he described in pantomime my flight across the room. He touched the wires in his enthusiasm, and it was my turn to smile.

Suddenly they stopped laughing and we all looked at each other in an embarrassed silence. I got them to sit down on the settee. It is a long one and they sat upright in the middle of it, father on the left, three children in the middle and mother on the right – dead straight like a row of blond tulips. I stood before them and tried to explain that my wife was out shopping and we hadn't brought the children with us this time because we wanted to have some peace and quiet for a week on our own, doing absolutely nothing – a second honeymoon.

'Wife – Frau,' I began, making curves in the air in front of me, 'shopping.' I mimicked having a bag over my arm and picking articles from imaginary shelves.

The Dutch family burst into fresh laughter, followed by spontaneous applause. I smiled, secretly pleased at my efforts until I spotted Pedro out of the corner of my eye. He had his hand on his hip and was obviously doing everything I was doing. I decided to forget the second honeymoon bit. Obviously it was useless trying to communicate further. We sat and stared at each other for a while in silence. Then Pedro offered them drinks, which I thought was a bit much. 'Me get them,' I said, taking firm command of the situation, and falling over Pedro's tool box on the way to the fridge.

It was then that the telegraph boy arrived with the telegram. They come in small blue squares in Majorca – not the telegraph boys, the telegrams – and one has to be careful opening them or they fall apart and one finishes up with a handful of Scrabble letters.

'ESECOMBO PLEASE THONE AGGENT RE BROADSTAY OFFER QUESTEX R R PL 72' I read. 'Thone' obviously meant 'phone' and 'aggent' was equally certain to be 'agent'. Working on this theory 'Broadstay' had to be 'Broadway'. Broadway! I thought, that's exciting – I'd played there for a few weeks with *Pickwick* and I'd always wanted another crack at it.

'Importanto,' I said to Pedro, waving the telegram at him. 'Telephono at onceo.' He understood eventually and nodded. The Dutch family just sat expectantly, waiting for me to fall over something again. I pointed to the fridge and made the drinking motion with my hand. Pedro got the idea immediately and as I turned towards the door I heard the clink of bottles.

The nearest telephone was in Son Servera, three miles away, and though my journey there was full of expectancy, my return was equally full of despondency. The Broadway show turned out to be a Sunday concert in Broadstairs.

I had only been away for a half an hour, but that was plenty of time for Pedro to have drunk enough to be teaching the Dutch mother a Spanish flamenco. From the settee, the rest of her family provided a hand-clapping accompaniment.

'Olé!' cried Pedro as I arrived.

'Oh no!' I replied, snatching the bottle from his hand.

That was the signal for my wife to arrive.

'There's nice – having a party are we?' she said in a bright voice.

'Pedro's been fixing the light.' I pointed at the wall.

She looked. 'It's upside down.'

'It's an English fitting though, and he's not used to them.'

'Not used to German beer either, is he?'

I had to agree.

Myra turned to the Dutch family and by some means unknown to me engaged them in earnest conversation.

I went back out on to the patio and sat down in the deck chair – five minutes later it started to rain.

Hello, Sailor

'IT'S MUMPS,' said the doctor, standing back and surveying my five chins. 'I think,' he added. 'It's difficult to tell with a jaw-line like yours.' I nodded miserably, my jowls flapping with the motion.

'You'll have to be careful at your age,' he said knowingly.

I was then thirty-eight and still in my prime, comparatively speaking.

'Well, I've heard rumours about being impotent and all that when you get mumps as an adult. But I had them when I was a kid.'

'You've got 'em again,' laughed the doctor, too readily for my liking. 'Orchitis is what you have to watch out for. Swelling of the testicles. Don't want you walking about with your whatsits in a wheelbarrow, now do we?'

'What do I have to do, then?' I queried querulously.

'Lie very still in bed. Don't move around too much. And when the swelling has gone down take a holiday. Get out and find some sunshine.'

I looked out of the bedroom window. It was a wild March day and the rain was bucketing down.

The doctor paused by the door. 'Try a cruise – finest thing in the world for a convalescent. Sea air and sunshine will do wonders for you.'

Three weeks later I lay on my bunk aboard the *S.S. Antilles* as it fought a storm in the Bay of Biscay. The rain streamed across the portholes, and all things being considered I preferred having the mumps.

I had booked a state-room for a trip to Trinidad, calling at various ports along the way. Vigo, Guadeloupe, Martinique, Puerto Rico and Caracas. It looked great in the brochures, and my wife and two children, Jennifer and Andrew – we had two more later on which proves that I can lie still in bed when I have to – were delighted with the prospect.

The state-room was on the sun deck, and when we arrived in it we were very touched by the presence on the table in the middle of the lounge of an enormous vase of flowers from Eric Sykes, who had been staying with us for the weekend.

The first couple of days were delightful. The food was excellent, which was to be expected on a French ship, and the children, who were nine and five respectively, Jennifer being the elder, loved the excitement of being on board ship. The sea was calm and I was beginning to recover my lost strength.

Then came the storm. The first indication we had that the weather was going to be rough was when Eric's vase began to slide down the table. I rescued it deftly. 'Howzat?' I cried to Andrew. He responded by throwing up all over Jennifer who promptly did the same thing to Myra.

As we were cleaning up the mess an announcement came over the tannoy calling everyone to boat drill. I had read about it in the 'instructions to passengers' leaflet which was in the cabin when we first came on board. The sirens would sound and we had to follow the arrows to the boat station allotted to us. One member of the family would suffice, it said. It also stated rather firmly that life vests had to be worn.

By the time I had put my overcoat on and then managed to fasten all the tapes of the Mae West-type jacket over the top of it, I was beginning to feel pretty sick myself. The vase of flowers had made its umpteenth trip up and down the table, miraculously being fielded just in time by Myra, who had also managed to put the children to bed. The siren gave a blast which frightened the life out of me, and stewards started banging on doors in French. I turned to leave for my appointment with the boat station and got stuck in the door. Myra, who by this time was almost helpless with laughter, managed to push me out on to the deck.

Now, it's quite easy to get lost on board ship even when you're not burdened with a life jacket and your spectacles are not steamed over as mine were. Boat station M on C Deck was the place I was aiming for, but for some reason I kept taking the wrong turning and I eventually found myself in the crew's quarters. They all had a good laugh and directed me back up the stairs in French. When I eventually arrived at where I should have been, the group of passengers who would have had to share the lifeboat with me regarded my bulk with alarm. There were Gallic mutterings until someone made the observation that if we were ever shipwrecked and forced to take to the boats, I could keep my companions in fresh meat for quite a while. The remark was followed by good-natured laugher, but there was a little too much patting and pinching for my peace of mind. When the drill was over we were all invited to take a cup of hot consommé. I drank mine too quickly and was sick all over the deck.

Once we were out of the Bay of Biscay life wasn't too bad. The only trouble we had was removing my son Andrew from those parts of the ship where he was not allowed to venture – the bridge, for example. He was stopped only just in time from heaving a deckchair overboard. The old lady in it was the one who prevented his action. He was not a noisy child nor even a wilful one, but by God he was a bloody nuisance on board that ship.

We were all looking forward to our first landfall in the Caribbean, and I was determined to be there on deck with my cameras to shoot Guadeloupe from every conceivable angle. Our state-room was, as I have mentioned, right on the sun deck, and it was about half past five on a lovely morning when I heard the sounds of the ship's engines slowing. Without waking Myra and the children I festooned myself with all my camera gear and eagerly threw open the heavy door. It flew back against the side of the ship where it seemed to encounter some object. I peered around the door and found that I was looking at a tall thin man in a bathing costume holding his hands over his nose.

'Sorry,' I said, stepping on to his bare feet. He gave a muffled yelp and without saying anything more limped off towards the swimming pool which was further down the deck towards the stern. I shouted apologies to his retreating back, receiving a huge shrug of his stringy shoulders in reply. 'Ah well,' I thought, and started snapping away with gusto.

That day we went ashore eager to stretch our legs and had a fine time until we lost Andrew in a cane field. After an anguished hour rushing around, we found him sitting with a bunch of little locals chomping away on a piece of raw sugar cane. When we eventually got back on board he had a violent attack of diaorrhea. Then Jennifer, who dined at a different time from Myra and myself, burst into tears and refused to go down to the dining-room. We couldn't work out what was wrong, until through her sobs we realised that she was embarrassed because she didn't know how to say 'Pass the salt' in French. It took me half an hour with a French dictionary and a lot of pantomime to get her to go and eat her dinner. Myra and I had ours in the cabin; we were too bushed to face the rigours of dressing up.

The following morning we were due to dock at six o'clock in Martinique, and so at a quarter to six, determined not to miss the opportunity of photographing our arrival, I got myself dressed, hung the cameras around my person, headed for the door and flung it open. They say that lightning never strikes twice in the same place, but you've got to believe me when I say that I hit the same bloke again as I stepped out on to the deck. This time he hopped around for quite a while uttering French exclamation marks and the odd oath. 'Pass the salt' wasn't mentioned but 'merde' was. This time he appeared to have been hit on the side of his face. He was wearing only a bathing suit as he had done on the previous morning and was evidently on his way for his pre-breakfast swim. I managed to stammer out my apologies without stepping on his feet and he backed away, rubbing his cheek and shrugging his shoulders, quite a tricky thing to do when you think about it.

Martinique was colourful – to say the least – and we were very interested to learn all about the eruption of the volcano which had cost so many lives, but when you've seen one bit of lava you've seen 'em all. Andrew managed to behave himself on the trip ashore, mainly because I had threatened to throttle him if he didn't. In the evening we were informed that the following night we would be dining at the captain's table. 'That's quite an honour,' I said to Myra. 'By the way, which one is the captain?' I looked around the dining-room.

'I don't think he socialises much, keeps himself to

himself I'm told.' Myra, through her frequent visits to the hairdresser's shop, had become quite an expert on what went on on board.

'That makes it all the more exclusive then, our dining with the captain,' I said, swigging away at the red wine. 'I've got the sea in my blood. My great-grandfather was a master mariner. An old Cape Horner. Killed by a belaying pin, he was,' I continued, repeating an old family myth.

Myra studied me through hooded eyes. She reckoned I'd had enough wine.

'Nonsense,' I said, pouring another glass for myself.

An hour later as I heaved and retched over the toilet back in our state-room Myra remarked, not without compassion, 'You might have the sea in your blood, but that's claret that's coming up.'

The following morning we put into San Juan, Puerto Rico, and in spite of my aching head I gathered myself and my cameras together to photograph the arrival. Myra watched me from the bed. 'Don't get your Nikons in a twist,' she called as I opened the door. 'Very funny,' I said over my shoulder and promptly fell over my feet and sprawled on the deck. I heard a stifled laugh and looked up to see the thin stranger in the bathing suit, pressed against the side of the bulkhead. He was obviously waiting for me to make my entrance before he passed the door of my state-room. Twice bitten, thrice shy.

He stepped over me without so much as a 'Bonjour' and went on his way to the pool, shaking his head as he did so. I could not think of anything to say, strangely enough.

We went for lunch to the San Juan Hilton which was a very palatial place indeed. Flamingoes stilt-walked in the grounds and in the foyer a magnificent marble staircase led up to the first floor. Before we went in to eat Myra took Jennifer and Andrew up the stairs to the toilet, whilst I went to the bar and ordered a daiquiri. I had two of them and there was still no sign of the rest of the family. Then a pink toilet roll unfolded itself down the staircase. I watched, fascinated, as it was followed by Myra and a tearful Jennifer. There was no sign of Andrew.

'He's locked himself in the Ladies' and he won't come out. And he's throwing toilet rolls under the door.' Myra was at the end of her tether, and Andrew was at the other end. 'You'll have to get him out. He'll only listen to you.'

I went up the stairs to the Ladies' and then came back down again. 'I can't go in there. It's the Ladies'.' The two daiquiris had numbed my senses. 'Leave him in there, he'll come out when he's hungry.' I was all for having lunch, but no, Myra wanted us all to sit down together. Back we all went up the marble stairs.

'Come out this instant,' I shouted through the closed door, using my terrible voice.

A large blonde lady came out in a rush, wild-eyed and unbuttoned. 'What's wrong?' She seemed distraught.

'My son is in there,' said Myra. 'He won't come out.'

We were joined by more people who had been attracted to the scene by the laser-beam quality of my voice. Eventually a huge coloured housemaid appeared. We told her of our predicament and she smiled understandingly. She went into the toilet and emerged thirty seconds later with our recalcitrant son. 'Here he is,' she said, handing him over.

'How did you do it?' I asked, pressing a dollar bill into her hand.

'Easy,' she said. 'I just told him that if he didn't come out, I'd kill the little son-of-a-bitch.'

I shook her warmly by the hand. 'My sentiments exactly. What price Dr. Spock?'

From then on we had no more trouble with Andy. We only had to threaten him with the black lady from San Juan to get him to agree to anything.

That night we dressed for dinner, excited at the prospect of dining with the captain. I brushed up my schoolboy French with the aid of the dictionary and Myra put on what I thought was a rather unnecessary amount of perfume. There were cocktails before dinner in a bar adjacent to the dining-room, which was different from the one in which we normally ate. We were a bit late getting there because I took a wrong turning and by the time we arrived our fellow diners were moving in to the table. I snatched a quick Scotch from a passing tray and escorted Myra towards our seats.

The Purser stood at the table ready to introduce us to the captain, this elusive man we had not yet glimpsed on the voyage. He had his back to us and there was something horribly familiar about those shoulders, even in gold epaulettes.

'Monsieur et Madame Secombe,' said the Purser.

The captain bent low over Myra's hand and straightened up to shake mine. His eyes opened wide in surprise. 'Vous!' he exclaimed, touching his bruised cheek.

'Oui, me,' I said fatuously, hoping that the floor would open up and swallow me.

'We 'ave met already,' he said grimly to the Purser and excluded me from the conversation from then on.

We flew home from Trinidad. It seemed the best thing to do under the circumstances.

Chlistmas Gleetings flom Singapore

CHESTNUTS ROASTING ON an open fire, the strains of 'Hark the Herald Angels Sing' filtering through the doors of a big department store, decorated Christmas trees in shop windows – a typical English city scene in December, you say? Wrong. It's Singapore. I am doing my Christmas shopping here this year and an exciting business it is. First allow me to fit another gin into my sling, lean on this passing coolie and digress a little on shopping in general.

Ever since I was a young lad staggering home on Saturday night from Swansea Market with the weight of my mother's shopping basket, I have been fascinated by shops. The reward for helping my mother home with the groceries was a fish and chip tea behind the market. And as there were many Saturday nights and many teas I have been programmed from my youth to equate shopping with food. My fixation is further strengthened by the fact that my father was a commercial traveller for a wholesale grocery firm and spent his life pounding the pavements of the back streets of the Swansea Valleys, refilling the little corner shops with supplies of baked beans, tinned soup, sacks of lentils, mounds of butter to be patted with wooden paddles, sides of bacon to be sliced to order, crates of tea to be emptied into large black jars labelled TEA and sold by weight on brass scales and wrapped deftly into packets by the shop-keeper before your very eyes. God – the nostalgia.

Strangely enough, even though I lament the passing of the little corner shop, I find the supermarket irresistibly attractive. I like nothing better than to take my trolley and trundle along the lanes of Sainsbury's in Cheam, laying waste to the shelves like Attila the Hun, until I get to the checkout counter where my wife relieves me of most of the items and I become Ethelred the Unready. There is an anonymity about supermarkets, too; no one bothers to look and say 'Hey, you are, aren't you?' and clutch you wildly by the arm.

This can be embarrassing, especially when those rallying to the call take a good close-up look at you and say things like 'He's better-looking on the telly' or 'He's never been one of my favourites'. They say these things as if one were not there. It usually takes a couple of choruses of 'Bless This House' to clear the shop and allow myself room to get to the counter.

Here in Singapore there is no chance of being recognised and I can enjoy the delights of anonymous shopping. There's every conceivable kind of shop here, selling everything one could ask for and some things one wouldn't dream of asking for – watches at four thousand pounds, for example. Most of the shops are in giant air-conditioned shopping complexes like the Orchard Road Shopping Centre or the one in Tanglin Road. Cameras, radios, watches, leather goods, radio cassette players, jewellery of every description, cram the window. This is a very prosperous city and the prices, alas, are not much different from those at home. There are bargains to be found, certainly, but beware of the cheap Omega watch, for instance. An Australian friend of mine bought one in Change Alley, a jam-packed passage off Raffles Place, loud with sound from radios and the voices of traders. He paid ten pounds for it and when he got on the plane to Sydney it fell apart on his wrist.

However, I have had one really good bargain. Last night I broke the right arm of my spectacles and this morning, in desperation, I asked a taxi driver to take me to an optician's. I was in and out of that place in ten minutes equipped with brand new frames costing only fifteen quid, and that's very cheap by any standards. Some of the best buys are in the Chinese Emporium in Orchard Road, where goods from Red China are sold alongside Western items. There was some lovely chinaware from Shanghai at a very reasonable price which I would have loved to have bought but I am notoriously bad at travelling with fragile goods. A beautiful selection of Oriental butterflies, framed and mounted, was on sale at less than five pounds. I have broken that already.

'You must get a suit made in Singapore, it only takes twenty-four hours,' a friend said to me. So I did. I went into a little Indian tailor's shop near the hotel and ordered a safari suit. It was welcomingly cool in the shop after the intense humidity outside and I gratefully accepted the glass of cold beer I was offered. An Indian gentleman invited me to choose the material from a large selection of cloth which filled shelves on either side of the tiny shop. When I had made my choice he began calling out my measurements to his assistant who had great difficulty in restraining his mirth. I was measured more thoroughly than I have ever been. Neck, inside leg, outside leg, waist to crutch, calf, thigh – I was beginning to think he fancied me. 'You will have your suit tomorrow, sir,' he said, doing an impression of Peter Sellers. I was unconvinced. 'Positive, five o'clock, sir.' I am still waiting, and my plane leaves at eight.

Last night I went shopping with a guide in the Chinese quarter. As soon as the sun goes down, out come the collapsible booths and the little side streets become instant market- places. The smell of roast chestnuts lured me to booths selling myriad varieties of Chinese delicacies – snake soup, shark's fin soup, tiger prawns. But live ducks and chickens waiting their turn for the pot turned me reluctantly away. In another alley were tiny one-man booths with a single working light where you can get your palm read, keys cut or your lighter mended. Fairy lights twinkling from canopies illuminated shirts, handbags, ties, dressing-gowns with embroidered dragons on them, shoes, cutlery, all the junk and gimcrack hardware of the Orient. Don't know how I'm going to pack it all.

P.S. My safari suit has just arrived... Imagine, only twenty-four hours ago it was just a large bolt of cloth. Now it has been transformed into a large bolt of cloth with buttons. It doesn't fit. It doesn't even touch.

Never mind, I'll just have to pack it into my suitcase. I press it down on top of the already cracked case of lepidoptera, which breaks completely and butterflies of every hue nestle among my clothes. A sudden thought strikes me. If they open my case in the customs and ask where I got the safari suit from, I shall say 'Moth Bros.'. The hotel porter wonders why I am laughing. So do I. One of my lenses has just fallen out. Melly Chlistmas.

Not Lost But Goon Before

IT IS MY experience, when travelling by air, that my luggage, in common with Robert Burns's 'best laid schemes o' mice an' men', gangs aft a-gley.

I once waited in vain in New York for baggage which, for reasons never properly explained, was down in Miami. It is reasonable to assume that one's luggage sometimes might feel in need of a change and would welcome the sunny left luggage office of a Florida airport to the icy blasts which sweep the Kennedy runways in late December. However, I was en route to Barbados at the time, where one would have thought that there was sun enough to suit the most cold-blooded of cases.

There must be a record for losing one's bags, and I'm sure I have to be in the running for it. I have left pieces of my personal equipment all over the world. Not a day goes by without something belonging to me winging its way in the wrong direction.

A small attaché case I had given up for lost in South Africa turned up unexpectedly in Perth, Australia. I had a telephone call at the theatre where I was playing, and a man who sounded as if he was trying to disguise his voice by a wearing a clothes peg on his nose asked me if I was indeed the H.D. Secombe whose name had been found under the lid. It took me a second or two to recall the item, and then I remembered losing a load of laundry which I had crammed into a case early one morning before leaving the hotel for Johannesburg airport six months previously.

'I'm afraid it does belong to me,' I said apologetically, realising that the caller at the other end of the telephone was in actual fact wearing a clothes peg on his nose. Cremation was the only way out, and now, since we have already quoted Burns, why not go the whole hog and paraphrase Rupert Brooke – 'There is some corner of an Australian field that is forever my laundry.'

Sometimes I feel – not like 'a motherless child', we've finished with quotations for the time being, thank you – that one's luggage takes on the character of its owner. To understand what I mean, just spend an hour or so watching people collect their luggage at Heathrow. Sleek brown Gucci-type matching cases invariably belong to sleek, tanned jet-setters; sensible, sturdy bags, multi-labelled, are plucked from the conveyor belt by chaps in tweed jackets with leather elbow patches; bursting cardboard boxes are rescued just in time by large West Indians; raffish, soft leather pieces are whisked away by furtive chaps in rakish caps, and strange, unclaimed items revolve endlessly like half-familiar stars in a 'Sunday Night at the London Palladium' finale, only to be claimed days later by me – and I leave the comparison to you.

Once you are sure that your cases have not been carried on the plane, the procedure is always the same.

Not Lost But Goon Before

You have to sort out the person in charge of the lost luggage department – this can take time if you are not conversant with the local language and the hour is late. There is a form which is in use at all airports. On it there is depicted every conceivable shape and size of case and you are requested to place a cross alongside the drawing which comes nearest to the piece or pieces you have lost. This can be difficult if you have indulged too well on the flight and are consequently unable even to remember the shape and size of your wife. It can lead to misunderstanding, and I still possess a large, square 'globetrotter' belonging to a lady of doubtful virtue, to judge from her underwear. She in turn must still be wondering what to do with the two check sports jackets and three pairs of flannel trousers which fell into her hands via my case, which was of a vaguely similar description. I saw recently a picture in a Spanish brochure of a donkey kitted out in something which looked suspiciously like one of my jackets – to be honest, it looked quite good on the beast. Which is more than I can say for the lady's underwear on me.

And that is something else I have to complain about. Whenever I lose my luggage I am always faced with the prospect of replacing some of the essential items within. This can prove a daunting task. I have only to put my nose near the plate glass window of any men's clothiers to bring the salesmen out with their hands up in surrender. My neck measurement is approximately the same as the average gorilla's – and as there is little chance of a gorilla, average or otherwise, dropping into the local haberdasher for the odd shirt or two, the demand for garments in my size is practically nonexistent.

Thus, when I was left in Barbados recently with only the suit I crouched in, and faced with the prospect of an indeterminate period before I saw my gear again, I saw red. However, before the authorities could bring in the man with the rifle to fire a tranquillising dart, my wife managed to talk me into a taxi to the hotel with the aid of a couple of bananas.

Once ensconced in my room I was unable to leave it in daylight for a swim in the inviting Caribbean. Topless bathing is accepted in certain parts of the island, but a bottomless bather is certainly not de rigueur! I was reduced to venturing into the sea in my underpants in the small hours before dawn, and then scurrying back to the room, Dracula-like, as the sun began to come up. This led to much talk of voodoo among the locals, and certain house-maids made the sign of the cross when we met on the stairs. I requested a Bloody Mary from room service one lunch-time and half the staff threatened to walk out.

Order was restored when my luggage eventually arrived via Montevideo, where it had been attending some conference or other. But it was a close call.

There's only one sensation to counter-balance the cruel realisation that the plane has not delivered one's creature comforts – or at least those that fit – and that is the one which accompanies the sight of one's baggage emerging through that hard rubber curtain of the conveyor belt, its labels wagging with pleasure and its battered sides heaving with the emotion of the reunion.

I began with a quotation and perhaps I should close with one. 'Everything comes to him who waits' they say, and that applies to lost airline luggage as much as it does patience, but, by God, you can grow old in the waiting, and so can your laundry.

Land of the Rising Damp

'Official opening today of a rain forest aviary at Taronga Zoo was washed out.

Minister for Lands, Mr. Lewis, who was to perform the opening ceremony, went to a tailor to be fitted for a new suit.' Sydney Sun, December 16, 1971

WHETHER MR LEWIS went to his tailor in a fit of pique, or because he had nothing else to do, or whether he had gone along early to the aviary and had the suit he was wearing christened by the birds, is a matter for fascinating conjecture. However, my reason for including this cutting is to demonstrate to the folks at home the kind of summer we're having here in Sydney.

A commuter also wrote to a local paper complaining to the Suburban Railways Department that the carriages on the trains were leaking. A spokesman for the Department replied that they were aware that the carriages leaked, but it was only troublesome when it rained.

Goon Overseas

'Write something on how to live under that wretched sun,' said the editor of *Punch* magazine when he discovered I was off to Australia. I nodded eagerly, my eyes already fixed on distant horizons, accepting the assignment in the spirit of a Stanley in search of an Antipodean Livingstone, my mind full of kangaroos, koalas and hot, burning beaches.

When I eventually landed at Sydney Airport, the sky was greyer than that over London when I left.

'You should have been here yesterday,' said an airport official. 'It was beaut.'

At least I think that's what he said. I had caught a cold in Hong Kong, and apart from violent spasms of sneezing I also had a blockage in my left ear. (It cleared quite suddenly three days later when I hit a top note in 'Bless This House' during a second-house performance in Adelaide – much to the surprise of the band who had finished playing and were on their way home. Thought you might like to know.)

On arrival at my hotel in Kings Cross the heavens opened, embracing me and my luggage. I entered the foyer with my tropical-weight suit plastered to my body and squelched my way to the Reception Desk.

'You're Harry Secombe,' said a lady nearby.

I smiled, warmed by the recognition.

'Why aren't you taller?' she demanded rather crossly.

'Try adjusting your horizontal hold,' I replied – cleverly, I thought – but she had gone.

In the lift the porter said, 'Should have been here yesterday. It was beaut.' He was on my good side at the time, so he definitely said it.

The sign on the landing outside my room said 'To the Swimming Pool'. I unpacked my luggage and sat on the bed in my bathing trunks waiting hopefully for the hot Australian sun to make an appearance. Four hours later I woke up shivering, my nose streaming with cold, and rain lashing the windows.

The house doctor was very sympathetic. 'You've got a touch of the "wog",' he said. 'Better stay in bed tomorrow.'

Of course, the sun came out in the morning, but all I got from it was sunburnt pyjamas.

The following day I felt better and was eager to sample the sunshine, but one look out of the window was enough. Rain and wind.

The commissionaire touched his cap as I stepped into the rainswept street.

'Shocking weather – you should have been here yesterday. It was beaut.'

'I was,' I said, splashing him playfully with drops from my bush hat.

Thus it has been since I arrived here. The warmth of Australian hospitality is tremendous; people have even loaned me their cars, something I've never known at home, and I've had so much free booze that my liver must resemble that of a Strasbourg goose. But nobody can turn on the sun. I spent a week in Adelaide, a lovely city with fine wide streets placed by its founder, Colonel William Light, on either side of the River Torrens, giving it a belt of parkland – a piece of town planning far ahead of its time. But I might just as well have been in Barnsley.

The cab driver from the airport had an answer for it. I opened the rear door of the taxi and got in.

'What's up, sport – have I got leprosy?'

I hurriedly got out again and sat beside him. We drove in silence through the rain until he said suddenly, 'The weather's got into the wrong hands. They're manipulating it, mate.'

I could only nod wordlessly, struck by the enormity of what 'They' were doing.

When he dropped me off at the hotel he said, 'Mind you, you should have been here yesterday.'

'I know,' I replied, 'It was beaut.'

'Nah,' he said, 'It was pissing down.'

At Brisbane the temperature was ninety degrees, but still no sunshine. However, heartened by the weather forecast, I bought a pair of shorts and some long white stockings and set off for the cricket ground to watch the World Eleven play the first match against Australia. I sat with some friends in the Members' Pavilion, the only one in shorts, like some monstrous Boy Scout at a lone Jamboree. The temperature dropped about fifteen degrees in no time at all, and the effect on me was so great that at one period the umpires sent a message from the field to ask who was playing castanets in the pavilion. Later that afternoon a thunderstorm of frightening intensity stopped play and traffic in one fell swoop.

I began to think that the travel brochures would have to be rewritten. Or perhaps it was always like this, that the fabled Australian sunshine was indeed a fable – a product of the Tourist Board. Maybe the cab driver in Adelaide was right, 'They' had somehow gained control of the weather. I went down with a bad cold again.

Back in Sydney I found that my old friend and fellow Army deserter Spike Milligan was in residence at Woy Woy, writing a sequel to his book book. I headed for Woy Woy on the next available train, to be hailed on my arrival at the station by a cry of 'I'm over here, you bloody Welsh Zulu.'

There stood my boon Goon companion, hardly recognisable in a floppy hat, over-long trousers and a shirt which would have been too big on me.

The rest of the day I can only remember in kaleidoscope. I vaguely recall digging in his mother's garden for Blue Tongued Skink; a wild drive up a hillside in the pouring rain to look at a Red Gum Tree he was fond of; two bottles of beautiful Australian burgundy disappearing along with Mrs. Milligan's curried chicken, and Spike deciding to start a Bell Bird sanctuary. This last decision resulted in a hilarious drive into the bush with a bewildered estate agent who was ordered to stop the car every few hundred yards while Spike got out to listen for the call of the Bell Bird. He bought an acre of land to which I was witness, although it might have been the other way around. That night the rain didn't bother me at all.

The weather has its compensations, though. I have been able to while away the hours watching television, which is on four channels and starts at seven in the morning and finishes about one a.m. At present the programmes are on the summer schedules, a time when the top shows take a holiday, and television becomes the Sargasso Sea of the cinema. All the films ever made seem to have drifted here and wallow sluggishly behind the screen. I swear I saw Finlay Currie as a young man one night last week – and even more appalling, I saw myself as a flickering fool in a film which I had fervently hoped had been cut up into celluloid collar stiffeners years ago. The last time I had heard of it, it was doing well in Afghanistan where, I believe, they are allowed to fire at the screen.

Wherever I have performed here I have met many 'poms' who are always anxious to hear news from home. One gentleman with as strong a Welsh accent as ever I have heard came back-stage to see me.

'When did you leave home?' I asked, thinking he was fresh from the boat.

'Twenty years ago, boyo,' he said.

It is very interesting to listen to the various accents here. Scottish, Irish and Welsh immigrants seem to retain their old way of speaking, and the stronger Northern dialects survive almost intact. On the other hand, I met a fellow I could have sworn was a 'dinki-di'

Australian, until after a few drinks he let slip the fact that he came from London twenty years ago, or whenever the Great Train Robbery was.

Tomorrow my family arrive from England and I shall be there at the airport to meet them. The weather forecast is 'showers, heavy at times', so if it's raining when they arrive I've got my greeting ready.

'You should have been here yesterday. It was beaut.'

On Being Ill Abroad

MY PROFESSION AS an entertainer allows me to travel as freely around the world as my passport photograph, which resembles a lunatic, will allow. In the process I think I have picked up more bugs and viruses than most people. For example, I've had mumps in Manhattan, bronchitis in Brisbane, tracheitis in Tasmania, broken an arm in Bermuda, perforated my bowel in Barbados and had pneumonia in Pnew Zealand. It only remains for me to leave my heart in San Francisco and I'll have done the lot. I therefore feel fairly well qualified to sound off on the subject of being ill abroad.

I have gleaned information on the different ways doctors behave. In America, for instance, it is almost impossible to get a general practitioner to make a house-call. A death-rattle over the phone is about the only way to winkle him out of his surgery. Then when you're cured and you see the amount he has charged, the death rattle starts up again.

There was a time in Taormina, Sicily, when I was seized with a particularly nasty virus which had the proprietors of the hotel worried in case it was contagious. They went to great lengths to see that I was comfortable and that no visitors dropped in to see me, apart from my wife, of course, whose meals they served at a table well away from the other guests. The doctor who came to look me over was a happy-go-lucky character who told jokes in bad English as he inserted a suppository. When I cried out rather sharply during the insertion he clapped me on the backside in admiration. 'Top C. You are tenore, si?' When I weakly admitted the fact he launched into a full-throated rendering of 'O Sole Mio'.

It was a strange serenade, because I remained on my knees with my head on the pillow as he had instructed. My wife had to thrust a handkerchief into her mouth to keep from laughing. He pocketed his fee with all the alacrity of a head waiter, kissed Myra's hand and departed before I could turn over. It's an experience I shall never forget – and I shall never be allowed to do so, either.

We have a pied-à-terre in Majorca where we always go for the children's school holidays, and one Easter time a special kind of virus stalked the island. The locals call most illnesses they don't understand the 'gripe'. Well, this bug didn't just 'gripe', it took you by the throat, threw you on to your back and jumped up and down on your chest.

The weather at Easter is traditionally bad in Majorca, and that year was no exception. The resorts were crammed with grim-faced tourists wearing raincoats, trudging from café to souvenir shop to bar and back again, paying a fortune for two-day-old English newspapers and generally wishing that they were back in sunny Barnsley again. The virus spread from contact;

the extra whisky to drive away the blues gave a sense of well-being and consequently those idiots who frequented the over-crowded bars came down with the 'gripe'. Of course, I was the first to get it.

Myra sent for the doctor, who happened to be a young lady fresh from medical school. The symptoms were explained to her by Magdalena, our Mallorcan house-keeper, and the doctor, having said 'Bueno' to everything Magdalena said, prescribed suppositories and injections. At least she didn't offer to do the job herself, or sing me a snatch from *Carmen.* It transpired that my wife had to do the necessary.

This caused great hilarity in my progeny, David and Katy, because they found their mother practising using the needle on an orange. Water melons were not in season. After a few tries she got it right, and my posterior, though raw, was duly injected. Within a couple of days I was as right as the rain which still fell in a steady drizzle.

But no sooner was I returned to the fold than my wife and her father went down with the virus. Now, Myra only takes to her bed to have children, and the house was thrown into utter confusion. Only Magdalena, who worked from nine in the morning to one o'clock, knew how to run things. I was like a chicken without a head. Katy and David, six and twelve respectively, felt bereft; David, remembering the last time his mother had stayed in bed, thought that yet another brother and/or sister was on the way; Katy was desolate because no one would play 'I spy with my little eye' with her. Then Magdalena fell victim to the dreaded lurgi and I was Florence Nightingale, Doctor Spock and short-order cook all rolled into one.

My wife was upstairs in our bedroom wanting only to be left alone, the two children shared a room downstairs wanting to be entertained, and my father-in-law, God bless him, with no desire to be any trouble to anyone, also had a bedroom on the main floor. The first day after Magdalena took sick was chaotic. Injections here, a suppository there, 'I spy with my little eye' through gritted teeth, a futile attempt to explain the Pythagoras Theorem to David; burned toast, burned baked beans and rubbery fried eggs for supper for the children and myself. The invalids were only interested in liquids. Myra wanted nothing and slept most of the time, only waking for medication, and Jim, my father-in-law, felt the same, although I had been warned that the antibiotics might be a little strong for someone of his advanced years. He was getting on for eighty at the time.

The second day things were running more smoothly –

the children were taken out for lunch by sympathetic neighbours and I was feeling that perhaps, after all, I could see the nursing period through without too much trouble.

That night at about half past twelve I heard a dreadful banging and crashing downstairs. I got up and made a quick search. Nothing had moved in the children's room and all seemed quiet in Jim's bedroom – until I realised that he was not in it. Nor was he in the bathroom adjoining it. However, from a deep cupboard directly opposite his room came loud thrashings and Welsh oaths. I opened the door and released my father-in-law. He had mistaken the cupboard in which we kept all the Christmas decorations for the toilet. He was festooned with stale Christmas cheer; spangles shone in his hair and fairy lights hung down from his shoulders. I took his hand gently, because he was a gentle man, and drew him from his temporary lair. 'A merry Christmas to you,' he said solemnly. I bade him a happy New Year and conducted him to his bed.

The following day was not too bad – Myra was still not really aware of what was going on, and Jim slept the day through, apart from the times when his injections were due. By this time I was a veritable William Tell with the needle. Too good, really, because I confused the doses and gave poor Jim more than he should have had.

When I went in to see him that night he was sitting bolt upright in bed. Previously he had been all but obscured by the blankets, his eyes closed and apparently dead to the world. 'What do you want for supper?' I asked, disturbed by the glint in his eye.

'I'll have what they're having over there,' he said, pointing to the far left-hand corner of his bedroom.

'Ah, yes,' I replied, cleverly playing for time.

'Those people over in the corner. I would like what you've just given them.' He was polite but firm.

113

'Where do you think you are, Jim?' I thought I might as well establish a common meeting-place.

'In a Chinese restaurant, of course,' he said with the air of one explaining to a child.

Now, I knew that my father-in-law had never set foot in a Chinese restaurant in his life. However, I decided to humour him and promised to return with whatever the people at the other table were eating. I went into the kitchen, made some tea and toast and brought it back to him. He ate it without speaking a word. When he'd finished he said, 'What did you have?'

'The same as you,' I replied.

'Bloody terrible, wasn't it?' he said and lay back on the pillow with his eyes closed.

The following morning I went down to his room to see how he was getting on, apprehensive about what mental state I would find him in. To my relief he greeted me quite normally.

'Feel much better today, son.' The glint was gone from his eye.

'Thank God for that,' I said.

'Aye. I think the old fever's gone now. I'll have a boiled egg for breakfast with some bread and butter.'

'Right you are, Jim.' I turned towards the door, happy that the old chap was back with us again.

'Hey,' he called, as my hand reached for the knob, 'they took a bloody long time to serve us last night.'

It was a week before Myra and Jim were fit to travel home, and it was a smiling Secombe family that boarded the plane. David and Katy sat in the seats in front of us. I leaned over the top of Katy's head to help her to fix her seat belt.

'Myra, have a look at this,' I said. 'Behind her ears. What are those spots?'

My wife looked long and hard. She sighed deeply. 'Measles, that's what they mean.' Then she looked behind my ears and said, 'You've got it too.'

But then, I had to, didn't I? Measles in Majorca. I don't just get ill abroad, I also suffer from global alliteration.

Goon on the Boards

Look Out Behind Yer!

"OH DEARIE ME," said Abenazar, a thin film of sweat gathering below the greasepaint-stained edge of his turban. He made yet another desperate gesture with his hands and still the expected flash did not appear from the area behind the centre footlights. The audience, composed mainly of tough Merseyside children, sat forward on their seats like a mob watching a Tyburn hanging, prepared to do the job themselves if necessary. The magician turned to them for mercy. Seeing none, he uttered the following immortal lines, sealing his fate with audience and management alike: 'Goodness gracious, what a caper, the cat's pissed on my magic paper.'

I was not actually present at that memorable performance but it is a legend in our profession and an experience with which I can easily identify. There's nothing quite as blood-curdling as the sound of children's excited voices coming over the tannoy system in the dressing-room as you are girding your loins to brave the first panto matinée of the season. It's like going out to face the Dalton Gang with a banana in your holster.

The evening performances are different – adults are there to play to and innuendo is appreciated. But stark reality stalks the matinée and a faint heart never wins a five-year-old audience. I know because I've lost a few myself.

My first pantomime was *Dick Whittington,* in which I played Dame with disastrous consequences, and when, some two years later, I was asked to play in *Jack and the Beanstalk,* I turned white. It was only when my agent whispered the magic words 'X pounds' in my ear that I reluctantly agreed. I was told to present myself at a church hall on the North Side of Clapham Common for rehearsal. After inadvertently attending a parish council meeting – which, upon subsequent reflection, had far greater comic potential than the pantomime I was in search of – I found the right place. The stage manager was waiting for me at the door. 'The producer's waiting for you,' he sniffed. 'He's in there, you can't miss him.'

He was right. The producer had a featureless face like a knee cap with nostrils. He wore a large teddy bear coat draped over his shoulders and a trilby hat perched rakishly over one eye. As I tiptoed into the rehearsal room, nervous at being late, he spotted me.

'Ah, Simon!' he boomed.

'No, Secombe,' I said apologetically.

'I know that, laddie. Simple Simon. That's what you are in the pantomime and that's what you are to me at rehearsal. Simple Simon.' He introduced the rest of the cast. 'That's Daisy the Cow.' Two middle-aged gentlemen sitting at opposite ends of a settle bench nodded perfunctorily. He lowered his voice to a shout. 'They're not talking to each other.'

Jack, in a fur coat, switched on a smile; Mary, in

trousers, gripped my hand firmly; the Giant looked embarrassed; the Broker's Men took time off from chatting up the chorus girls to greet me, and the Dame, a little man with eyes like blackcurrants, offered me a wine gum. I took a red one.

I was handed a script and we began reading. There was no mention of Simon for the first few pages and I sank into a reverie.

'That's you, Simon,' said the producer sharply, breaking into my private world.

'It says "Frankie" here.'

'Ah yes, that was last year when Frankie Howerd played Simple Simon. Read it.'

'Ladies and gentlemen – oooh – ah – yerss. Now then, missus.' I put the script down. 'I can't say this – it's all Frankie Howerd's patter.'

The producer tipped his hat back on his head. 'Put it in your own words then.'

I shifted uncomfortably. 'Well, I always start off my act with my own catch-phrase.'

'Say it then, Simon, and we can all get on.'

I swallowed hard. 'Well, hello there,' I said lamely. 'That's how I always start my act on "Variety Bandbox". Then I do a raspberry and a little giggle.' My voice got smaller as I explained.

'That's it, is it? We need at least three minutes there for Jack to change.' The producer's hat went further back.

'I'll come in there if you like.' The Dame was very helpful. He was equally helpful every time there was a gap which I was supposed to fill. By the time the show opened he was hardly ever off the stage, and during the interval the bastard threw sweets into the audience.

'Fee-fi-fo-fum,' said the Giant, making it sound like an invitation.

The producer threw his hat on the floor. 'God's teeth!'

he roared. 'Now I've seen everything. A camp bloody giant.'

Rehearsals continued and in spite of everything we opened without too many mishaps. During the run of the show I learned a lot about working with other actors, as opposed to doing a solo variety act. I was upstaged so often by the Principal Boy that I found myself addressing most of my lines to the conductor. At one matinée the Cow seemed about to rend herself asunder as muffled explosions and audible oaths came from inside her skin. We gathered later that the front end had got his own back on the rear end by drinking four pints of draught Bass before the performance. The Broker's Men had most of the chorus, the wardrobe mistress and Mary were seen holding hands, and the Giant found someone friendly in the flies. All in all, an ordinary run-of-the-mill pantomime.

I have been in many pantomimes since then – so many that I have had kids who played the babes in *Babes in the Wood* bring their own children backstage to meet me. But of all the shows I have done, *Humpty Dumpty* was my favourite. We played a season at the London Palladium and the following year at the Palace, Manchester. It was there that I was involved in the greatest transformation scene ever witnessed.

Every weekend I travelled down to London by sleeper on Saturday night and flew back on the Monday morning plane. One unforgettable Monday, the plane was delayed – not enough to worry about at first, and Tommy Cooper, who was playing the Opera House, Manchester, was a most amiable companion at the bar. The delay continued until it was obviously going to be too late for me to get to the theatre in time for curtain-up. I rang the Palace and told them to put my understudy on. For some strange reason my stand-in was a diminutive lady of slight build who doubled as Mother Goose, and could easily have fitted into the left leg of my costume. Anyway – on she went.

Meanwhile, back at Heathrow, Tommy Cooper was in the middle of performing his celebrated 'Eskimo taking a leak' impression using a handful of ice cubes as props, when our flight was suddenly called. I was met by a distraught manager at the airport and driven like the clappers to the theatre.

I arrived half-way through the first half, dressed in thirty seconds flat and got to the wings at the very moment that Betty Jumell, my understudy, was about to make her re-appearance on stage after being turned from a chicken into a human being – in the panto, that is. I thanked her hurriedly and ran on stage.

The gasp of astonishment from the kids which greeted my appearance was tremendous. The transformation was so great that there was a deathly hush for at least five minutes. And for pantomime that's a supreme achievement.

It wasn't so good for Tommy Cooper at the Opera House, though – his props had melted.

From Parlour to Palladium

THERE WAS ONCE an American night-club comedian who used to come on stage, glare at his audience and begin his act with the immortal words, 'Good evening, opponents.' It takes a brave man to do that, believe me. Those of us who spend our lives trying to coax laughter from reluctant throats might often feel like using similar tactics, but we would have been lucky to leave the stage of the Empire, Glasgow on a Friday night second house in one piece.

We comedians *have* to love our audiences just as much as we want to be loved in return. In the dressing-room before I go on I always pace up and down wondering how they are going to be out there. I think of them crouching in the darkness waiting for me to appear, hoping that they are going to love me as much as I want to love them, and at the same time asking myself why I took up performing in the first place.

What makes us go on stage and make fools of

ourselves? It's not just the money. It has to be exhibitionism in some form or another – a desire to show off, to be noticed, to be loved – and it usually reveals itself at a fairly early age.

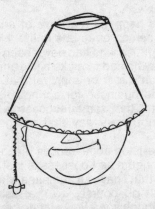

A budding comedian is the child who likes to dress up in his father's clothes and wear a lampshade on his head at family get-togethers. (The boy who prefers to put on his mother's frocks and lipstick has a different kind of problem with which we should not concern ourselves here.) He draws attention to himself in this way and if he is lucky he will be rewarded by laughter and a little light applause. This spurs him on to greater efforts and he begins to seek wider horizons and larger lampshades. The four walls of the front parlour can no longer contain him, and his desire for acclamation might drive him on to the stage of the Church Hall.

If his lampshade act goes down well there he will be so excited by the applause that he is usually hooked for life. 'All those people out there are laughing at *me*,' he thinks. 'I love them, I love them.' He spends all his pocket money on lampshades for his act, and when he grows up he becomes a light comedian. It's as simple as that. A clip around the earhole from his father when he first donned a lampshade might have stopped the rot, but once he has heard that laughter and applause, there is no turning back.

It sometimes happens that love of an audience can take hold of a person quite late in life. I know a theatre manager in his fifties who had never been on stage in his life until one day he had to make a live announcement. It earned him such a roar of approval that he forsook his own side of the business for acting. Unfortunately he never met with the same success again because, naturally, it's not every day that we get Germany to surrender.

Constant television appearances mean that someone with as large a figure as I possess is instantly recognisable, and I find that I have an audience wherever I go. It is a compliment, of course, to be asked for one's autograph, although sometimes it can be rather inconvenient. I was once spotted entering the gents' toilet in one of the motorway garages and was forced to sign pieces of paper thrust under the door by a party of children on a school outing. Some of them were girls.

In Majorca I was once having my hair cut in a barber's shop in the main street of Cala Millor. There was no one else in the place and I was having the full treatment – shampoo, massage, and the bit where they put a net over your head and dry your hair with a blower. Rather decadent but very relaxing. The shop has a large plate glass window and people were wandering about the street outside. Out of the corner of my eye I saw passing a middle-aged man wearing the unmistakable British holiday gear – short-sleeved Celanese shirt, sandals with socks and khaki shorts. His wife was wearing a mac.

They walked out of sight and after a short pause they came back again. The woman peered at me through the glass and nodded to her husband. He in turn shook his head. She then called to someone out of vision and suddenly the window was full of people, some nodding their heads, others shaking them. They seemed to reach a decision and delegated one of their number to open the door. He was a short, bald man with an aggressive manner. Putting his face up against mine he scrutinised me carefully and then, without saying a word to me, he called back to the others who were now crowding the door – 'It *is* him!' I waved feebly at them.

The barber, who was at first nonplussed by this invasion, carried on with his job while I tried to look unconcerned. The crowd outside began shouting encouraging remarks to him as he swivelled my neck this way and that. Slowly he began to respond to his unexpected audience and he put on a show for them. His success went to my head. He removed the net, flourished his comb and scissors and snipped away at my nostril hairs, getting a round of applause for his delicacy of performance. Powder and hair oil flew in all directions as he completed his ministrations. By this time I, too, became involved, and sang a little snatch from *The Barber of Seville*. 'Bravo!' cried our audience. The barber whipped the sheet from around my neck like a matador doing a fancy pass with his cape, whisked the hairs away with a brush, and we both bowed to the storm of applause.

It was one of the most bizarre experiences in my life. It was also one of the worst haircuts I have ever had, but that's neither here nor there. The audience loved it and that's all that matters, really, isn't it?

Pickwick

THE IDEA OF PICKWICK as a musical came to me in Barbados in the Christmas of 1961. I had just finished an arduous season at the London Palladium – or the Fun Factory, as we call it – and was taking a holiday in the sun. For some months I had been trying to find a suitable musical subject for myself – quite difficult, really, in view of my size. I am not exactly a romantic lead, and my voice is not a drawing-room tenor – it's more of an 'outside on the verandah' type, glass chandeliers being in short supply.

So there I was, idly fixing myself a rum punch, when the mail arrived. In it was a letter containing a cutting from the Christmas edition of *TV Times*, with a photograph of myself as Father Christmas in the 'Jo Stafford Show' which went out on Christmas Eve. Looking at it, I remembered the scene in the show where I played a Dickensian-type landlord, and suddenly I thought of myself as Pickwick. As fate would have it,

Wolf Mankowitz came for lunch that day, and I
mentioned the idea to him. He liked it and said he would
do the book adaptation.

I went back to London full of the idea and approached
Bernard Delfont, who also was fired with enthusiasm.
The question then was, who was to do the lyrics and
music? Leslie Bricusse's name was mentioned as
lyricist because of the success of *Stop the World,* and
Cyril Ornadel was suggested as the ideal composer for
the job because he knew my voice and was also capable
of listening to it flat out without wincing. I found out later
that he was wearing ear-plugs. Peter Coe was approached to direct the show in view of his great success
with *Oliver!* and so was Sean Kenny, who was the scene
designer for the same show.

So we had a team together for the job and the first
task was Wolf Mankowitz's. How much of *The Pickwick
Papers* to leave in, and how much to leave out? The book
was written as a serial and is essentially episodic. The
difficulty was going to be deciding what peg to hang the
action on. It was resolved, after much deliberation, to
concentrate on the Bardell misunderstanding, which
gave us the Fleet Prison scenes in both halves and a
good big courtroom comedy scene in the second act. It
was a difficult decision, and we had to take a lot of
chronological liberties with the book. However, on closer
examination we discovered that Charles Dickens himself
was not too sure about the exact order of events. For
example, although the events of the Pickwick Club are
set firmly in the year 1827, with the meeting of the Club
on May 12th, when we come to June 2nd – the time of the
Eatanswill Election – we find Mr. Pott directing Jane to
bring him the file of the Gazette for 1828, the file, of
course, being the one for the preceding year, which
makes the year in which it was called for 1829.

Again, Winkle and Tupman reached Bury on the

evening of September 13th and while at dinner they receive Dodson and Fogg's notice of action dated August 28th 1830! Then again, after Sam's visit to Dorking on September 8th and 9th we get the party separating for a 'short time', each going home to prepare for a Christmas visit to Dingley Dell. Even the most elaborate preparations should not have taken more than a month at the outside, which would bring us to the middle of October. However, we find the Pickwickians starting off on December 22nd in the year of grace in which these, their faithfully recorded adventures, were undertaken and accomplished. So we are back again from 1830 to 1827. And the best of Dickensian luck!

To return to the musical, we eventually went into rehearsal in April, 1963, prior to our opening in Manchester in June. A lot of time was spent studying models of the four mobile trucks which were to form the scenery for the production. They were to be handled in full view of the audience by the actors themselves, who in consequence had to become assistant stage managers as well – union rules, of course. So we were to have the extra hazard of the possibility of being run over in mid-song. In addition I had to learn to skate for the Dingley Dell scene, a prospect viewed with some alarm by my agent as it entailed my dropping through a prepared hole in the ice as the finale to the first act. 'Danger money' began to be suggested by some of the company – led, of course, by myself.

It is all a bit kaleidoscopic in my mind now. I remember the first time we heard the music played by the orchestra after weeks of rehearsal with just piano, and the wonderful feeling of excitement we experienced. I remember the costume fittings when Bermans sent my measurements back, saying they must be a joke.

All the time we were getting to know each other as a company, and particularly the members of the Pickwick

Club itself – we began to feel an affinity with each other. Julian Orchard as Snodgrass was to prove a tower of strength throughout the run; Oscar Quitak as Winkle had a gentleness of manner which endeared him to us all, and Gerald James as Tupman was a fellow Welshman – need I say more? Peter Bull as Buzzfuz provided us with many sly laughs, and Jessie Evans as Mrs. Bardell, the only lady baritone in captivity, kept driving the conductor mad with her variations of the tune she had to sing. There were minor clashes of temperament between the writers and musicians – no show has ever been put together without them – but I can honestly say that we on the acting side never had any words at any time. It seemed as if the spirit of old Samuel Pickwick reached down and touched us all.

When we eventually opened in Manchester we over-ran by some twenty minutes and there were a few changes to be made here and there, but we all felt that with luck we had a hit on our hands. A month of hard work followed – rehearsals every day and a show at night, two with matinées. Slowly I began to find myself more at home in the role. It was difficult at first tackling a character so firmly fixed in everyone's minds by the illustrations of Seymour and Phiz, and so universally loved. My initial worry was how much of myself to allow to creep into the portrayal, and how much I should subdue my natural instinct for broad comedy. In the end I found that after the first few minutes the audience got over the shock of seeing Neddie Seagoon in a bald wig, and settled down to watch Samuel Pickwick, Esq. Occasionally I was tempted to play a little more broadly than was intended, but on the whole I managed to control myself. But it should always be remembered that the old gentleman was a clown in many respects and, like the other members of the Club, essentially larger than life – or at least life as we know it today.

We opened at last in the West End at the Saville Theatre on July 4th, and we all felt at the end of the opening night that we had a hit on our hands. The critical reception the following day was fairly mixed. Milton Shulman approved of us; Herbert Kretzmer said it was a near disaster; the *Mail* said I was too subdued as Pickwick; the *Telegraph* said I was too extrovert. We took comfort from the fact that the original book was criticised quite severely by some. 'The Pickwickians', said the *Fraser* critic, 'are not furnished with a single gentleman-like accomplishment or possessed of a single gentleman-like feeling. As for honour, or pathos, or common sense, it must be wholly out of the question.' Said another, 'Pickwick's companions are very uninteresting personages, having peculiarities rather than characters.' My aim was to do justice to Pickwick and his essential humanity, summed up by a contemporary critic as 'a most amiable and eccentric combination of irritability, benevolence, simplicity, shrewdness, folly and good sense, frequently ridiculous but never contemptible'.

We come now to Chapter Two: How the members of the Pickwick Club fared on their journey to the New World; how they resisted all attempts at sabotage; how they stood valiantly together on Broadway, and sundry other interesting and revealing items.

Having had a very successful season at the Saville Theatre in spite of Herbert Kretzmer, we were approached one day by a Mr. David Merrick, an impresario from across the water (who gave the impression that he might have walked across), with a view to performing in the New World. 'Harry,' he said, 'you're the eighth wonder of the world' – a statement which had me flipping through the *Encyclopaedia Britannica.* Perhaps he meant a cross between the pyramid of Cheops and the Colossus of Rhodes. He tempted us with money and so we decided to chance our fortune – with some trepidation, I might add, having in mind the unfortunate experiences of Charles Dickens himself in America.

After much haggling with American Equity, most of the principal characters headed for New York for rehearsals. I joined them later in San Francisco in time to learn the new scenes which were being introduced to make the show more palatable to American audiences. A mistake, I might add. New songs and lyrics were thrown in, and just as quickly tossed out again. Even after we had opened we were still experimenting. The stage was full of written cues on the footlights and on the backs of *hands, none of which was exactly conducive to a relaxed performance.

The San Francisco opening, incidentally, was a great success, and we all thought that we were heading for a long Broadway run. The young lad playing Sam Weller until Roy Castle was able to take over, later became famous as Davy Jones of the Monkees, and very good he was, too. We had seven weeks in San Francisco and then down to Los Angeles where we did another seven week run in a theatre so vast and ornate that I told the manager, 'If we get the bird here, at least it will be a peacock.' We found we had to slow down the speed of our dialogue considerably for the audiences there, something which I found quite difficult at first. But on the whole we were delighted to find that the comedy was even better received than it was in London – the visual comedy particularly. The critics were fairly kind to us – one said, 'The show, by Chuck Dickens, looks pretty good.' Another said that I was the nearest thing to Ionesco's bald soprano he had ever heard or seen.

Slowly we worked our way nearer New York and Broadway – probably the longest out-of-town tour ever, six months. We played Cleveland and lost, Detroit for a month, where the wig came off during my cartwheel and I had the presence of mind to shout 'Indians', a sally received in total silence by the matinée audience. We had standing ovations in Washington and we all thought we would lay Broadway on its ear. Finally we got to the 46th Street Theatre, after resisting many attempts to Americanise the show with inserted songs like 'You'll always find a chap'll slap your back and slip you ten' and an American Tupman who insisted on saying 'every last nickel'. We did four charity previews before the real opening, which coincided with the visit of the Pope and a newspaper strike.

The reviews, when they did come out, were good, some extremely good, but Taubman and Kerr, the two butchers of Broadway, were not complimentary. This had an adverse effect on the box office advance although we played to very good business for the seven weeks we were there. The decision to close the show came when I was ill in bed with mumps, and the first indication I had of it was when I read it in the paper – 'last eight performances'.

Everyone was taken by surprise, especially as we finished the last week to standing-room only business. Still, no one can afford to lose money to the extent it can be lost on Broadway, and David Merrick, having made a handsome profit on tour, was not prepared to gamble it for the few weeks prior to Christmas, a bad time of year for shows. However, we finished on a very high note and I can honestly say that we did not tarnish the memory of the immortal Samuel Pickwick or his creator.

There, then, is the saga of the musical, an experience I would not have missed for all the money in the world. All of us connected with the stage adventures of the Pickwick Club felt, at the end, humbler and better men by our association with the works of Charles Dickens.

The Spice of Life

BRING BACK THE birch, I say. June Birch, the lady trumpeter. Let's see once again the Wilsons, Keppels and Bettys of yesteryear. Before I go into a decline, come with me down memory lane but be careful how you tread, this is Lurgi the Wonder Dog territory.

When I left the army my first job was at the Windmill Theatre. Out of the frying pan and into the foyer, as one might say if one dared. 'Revuedeville' they called the shows there because they were a combination of decorous dancers in diaphanous dresses, showgirls wearing nothing but strategically-placed sequins and fixed smiles, and raw comedians like myself doing solo acts... a rare mixture of revue and variety. It was not until some months later, when I played the Grand Theatre, Bolton, that I first came into contact with the real variety theatre, or music hall as it was called then.

I was one of the new breed of comedians spawned by World War II service concert parties, along with Max

Bygraves, Norman Wisdom, Tommy Cooper, Frankie Howerd, Benny Hill, Norman Vaughan, Michael Bentine, Peter Sellers, Spike Milligan, Dick Emery, Alfred Marks, Tony Hancock and Jimmy Edwards – only one of whom was there to help me on my opening night. Norman Vaughan was in the wings when I went on and he was helpless with laughter. At the time I was doing my shaving act which, very briefly, consisted of doing impressions of the way different people shaved, and I finished with a duet between Jeanette Macdonald and Nelson Eddy, both parts being sung by myself. First house Monday is traditionally bad in Variety. Landladies and local shopkeepers used to get complimentary seats and like all people who get something for nothing, were far from complimentary afterwards. I won't dwell on the reception I got – suffice it to say that I was lucky to make it off stage in one piece, leaving behind me a lynch-mob murmuring that stays with me to this day. The owner of the theatre paid me off in twenty-five one pound notes after that single performance, at the same time uttering the immortal words 'You'll not shave in my bloody time.'

Thus I was fired in the crucible of the provincial variety theatres, slowly being turned into the misshapen toby jug I have now become. There was comradeship in those days, though, a backs-to-the-wall bond against the common enemy – the audience. There were weird and wonderful acts to watch from the wings. Karinga and her Alligators, Mike Bentine doing marvellous things with the back of chair and a sink pump, foot jugglers lying on their backs and performing miracles with huge, red-painted barrels, and one act I will always remember. He used to finish his performance in a most spectacular way. He would put on a helmet with a spike on it and strap it under his chin, then when he was ready he would spread his legs wide and brace himself as a huge cartwheel dropped from the flies above the stage. He would catch it on the spike and spin it around and every time, if you were standing close enough to him in the wings, you could hear his heartfelt cry: 'Oh Jesus Christ!', as the wheel hit the spike.

Then there was an act called Rudy Horne, who did a fantastic routine on a unicycle. After juggling with about a dozen clubs he would balance himself in such a way that he was able, with one foot, to throw a saucer on to his head, followed by a cup, followed by another saucer and another cup until there were half a dozen cups and saucers on his head. As if that was not enough, he would then put a spoon into the top cup, still with his foot, mark you. And for his pièce de résistance he would finish by flicking up a cube of sugar to join the spoon.

I first saw him do this at a dress rehearsal at the Palladium. I was standing side-stage with Charles Henry, a dry-witted old 'Crazy Gang Show' producer. When the cube of sugar went into the cup he sucked his teeth in a deprecating way. 'He's not as good as he used to be,' he said, amidst all the applause from the pros out front. 'What do you mean?' I said. Charles scratched his nose. 'He used to use demerara,' he said.

It's a vanished world, though. Acts used to meet at Crewe Station on a Sunday because that was when we all seemed to pass through on our way up or down the country for the next week's engagement. Comics in camel hair coats would exchange gags solemnly in the buffet; conjurors would chat up chorus girls; singers would complain about the theatre acoustics and musicians would get drunk. A motley crew we were, with greasepaint on our collars and our props in battered suitcases. You don't see us on railway platforms any more because the business has changed. It's up the M1 in a car to play a one-night stand in a club where the supporting acts are a disc jockey and a group of musicians who believe that the louder they play the better they are, or a singer with a microphone halfway down his throat singing 'You Need Hands' and only using one.

Radio kept variety going in the 'thirties and after the war when, for a short time, there was a boom in theatre attendance. We comics all had our catch-phrases. 'Well hello there!' delivered in a high-pitched voice and followed by a raspberry was mine. God, when I think of it! 'Now listen,' was Frankie Howerd's; 'You lucky people,' was Tommy Trinder's. The listening public would pay to come to the theatre just to see what we looked like. If you weren't any good in the flesh you went once round the Empire circuit and fused yourself.

But just as radio gave variety a new lease of life, television came along and killed it. Once people could see their favourites in their own front room it became too much of an effort to leave the house and see them when they played the local theatre. So eventually speciality acts, who by performing on TV were giving away the work of a lifetime, drifted into continental theatres or the circuses, and the comics and singers went into the Northern clubs for personal appearances. The Empires and Hippodromes became bingo halls or were knocked down to make way for supermarkets.

I know I have taken a long time to get to it, but I would like to see variety back where it belongs, in a National Variety Theatre. It's too late to restore the old music halls so let us at least preserve the art form. Let's have a subsidised theatre where some of the marvellous speciality acts can teach their craft to others before they disappear for ever. A class for jugglers, perhaps – though I don't mean that we should breed a generation of flat-headed wheel catchers. A school where talented variety acts can pass on their skills, give aspiring comics a chance to play to audiences who are paying attention to them – not eating and drinking at the same time –

allowing them to get laughs without having to use four-letter words to shock people into listening. After all, if a ballet dancer can leap about in a truss paid for by the public, why can't a tap dancer do the same thing? We are all brothers under the leotard.

If you look at the long list of ex-service comedians I mentioned at the beginning of this piece, you may well think that it takes a war to produce a comic. Failing that, comedians have to practise in our parlours on television, making mistakes before millions and not hundreds. We can't have that now, can we? So come along now to the National Variety Theatre. . .seats in all parts.

Tony Hancock

COMEDY IS THE business of a comedian and laughter is the prerogative of his audience. It follows, therefore, that whereas a comedian must deliver his comedy, the audience does not have to give up its laughter. He is then, at the beginning of his act, in a state of conflict with his audience.

To understand a comic, one has first of all to analyse the requirements of his job. He must have a certain mental toughness, a quick wit, the ability to shrug off a bad reception, and at the same time possess the sensitivity to be aware immediately of the mood of his audience. Two options are open to him – either he gives them what he wants or he provides them with what they want. If he opts for the former he is liable to finish up returning to the rice pudding factory from which a talent scout plucked him.

Yet such are the vagaries of the comedy profession that in the days of radio, one catch-phrase repeated often enough by an indifferent performer could pervade the national consciousness and make him a star. The duration of his stardom depended upon his capacity to back up his gimmick with solid comic ability so that when the time came to cash in on his radio popularity in the theatre, his act had some kind of substance. The shrewd performer crying 'Open Sesame' as he rubs his magic lamp before the Aladdin's cave of show business should be careful to take out an insurance policy in the event of the non-appearance of the Genie. The comic David facing the Goliath audience has to be prepared with a song and dance routine in case his sling shot misses its mark.

Anyone who does a job of work and at the end of the day has nothing tangible to show for it, apart from his salary, has every reason to feel insecure. You can't frame applause, you can't place cheers on your mantelpiece and you can't plant a chuckle in a pot and expect it to raise laughs. All the average comic is left with at the end of his career are some yellowing newspaper cuttings, perhaps an L.P. or two, and a couple of lines in *The Stage* obituary column. But, if he is one of the few greats, he leaves behind a legacy of laughter when he has gone, especially – and such is human nature – if there has been an element of tragedy in his life. The public likes to think that there is drama lurking behind the laughter – agony caused, ironically, by the insecurity induced by the creation of the laughter.

Tony Hancock was one of those rare ones who are bedevilled by success. He was never completely happy in the variety theatre; the strain of repeating the same performance night after night and trying to invest it with an apparent spontaneity was more than he could bear. His timing and delivery were never better than when he was doing something fresh – creating and not re-creating. That was why he took to television so well, it removed him from the treadmill of the music hall and the twice-nightly revue and gave him new situations in which to work his magic.

Of the rampaging, drunken, self-destroying Hancock depicted in so many stories, I knew very little. I have drunk with him and been drunk with him in the days when we were both young and inexperienced comics fresh from the services, but it was all good-natured tippling then. The truth for which we were searching wasn't far away – it was there in the bottom of the glass.

Strangely enough, the time I remember Tony with most affection was when we were playing on the same bill at Feldman's Theatre, Blackpool in April, 1949. Out of season isn't the best time to be in a seaside town, and to make matters worse we were received with indifference by those who formed the small audiences. I was then doing my shaving act and Tony was doing his Gaumont British News impressions and some hesitant patter. On the opening night, Monday 11th April, at about ten past eight, I was rushed to the manager's office to receive a telephone call telling me that my wife had given birth to our first child, a daughter. I waited until Tony came off – he was further up the bill than I was – and told him the news. 'We'll celebrate, lad,' he cried.

We had about twelve shillings between us, and although champagne was out of the question, we were determined to wet the baby's head. It was a most frustrating night because by the time we had taken off our make-up the pubs had shut and the only place open was a fish and chip shop near the theatre. We sat together over our plates of frizzled rock salmon and toasted my first-born in Tizer – an aggressively non-alcoholic drink with a high gassy content. Later we wandered down to the sea front, drunk with the occasion and each other's company. We shared the same dreams of success and we argued about what we would do with the world now that we had fought to save it, leaning over the iron bars of the promenade, looking into the dark sea and seeing only brightness.

I met him many times later and at one time stood in for him on his radio show. But I will always think of Tony Hancock as he was then, pristine and shining with ambition at the threshold of his career. What happened to him subsequently is for others to chronicle and argue about. I found him gentle and self-mocking then. The demands of his profession shaped him, ground him down and eventually killed him, but he served it well. If anyone paid dearly for his laughs, it was the lad himself. May he lie sweetly at rest.

Goon on a Flight of Fancy

The Shattered Illusionist

BOB BARTLETT STOOD in the wings at the Palace of Varieties, Bradfield and watched his act getting the bird. It was not his act in the sense that he was a part of it – he was a theatrical agent who booked performers and referred to them when dealing with other agents as 'my acts'. This, however, was one for which he would gladly have disclaimed responsibility. It was a husband and wife team, although the wife got no credit in the billing. 'Mysto, the Eastern Illusionist' was all it said on the posters at the front of the theatre.

'Never been further east than Southend Pier,' said the stage manager who stood beside Bartlett waiting for the next cue.

'I know,' Bartlett said sadly. 'I booked him there – he nearly burned the place down with his fire-eating act.'

On stage Mysto, dressed in a long Eastern gown with a turban low over his forehead, was attempting to make two doves disappear. 'Voilà!' he cried in a broad Yorkshire accent, pointing a wand in the direction of a

147

very thin mousy-haired girl in a leotard and tights who stood near a black velvet table upon which sat the bedraggled birds. A flash went off behind him and the doves took off for the auditorium. 'Bloody hell fire,' said Mysto – born Arthur Lightfoot – despairingly.

'He's always doing that,' observed the stage manager. 'Gets everything mixed up.'

Bartlett nodded agreement. 'It's getting harder to find theatres to take him.' He shook his head and decided to wait for the act in their dressing-room.

The room was full of the paraphernalia of the stage illusionist. Fake bouquets of flowers were strewn in one corner and a large white rabbit glared at him from a small cage. Most rabbits are docile but Mysto, with his usual bad luck, had acquired one with a bad temper. In the middle of the room was a roughly-made chair with electrical wires trailing from it. An evening paper lay on the cluttered dressing-table and Bartlett picked it up. 'Hitler accuses Czechoslovakia' he read. Nineteen thirty-eight had seen many scare headlines featuring Adolf Hitler and Barlett wondered vaguely who his agent was.

The door banged open suddenly and Mysto stormed his way in. His wife followed hesitantly. 'The flash was in the wrong place again. If I've told you once I've told you a thousand times . . .' The magician took off his turban and threw it on the floor. Three stunned white mice crept out.

'Oh! Hello, Mr. Bartlett.' Mysto grinned awkwardly. 'Had a bit of a mishap with the doves.'

'I saw it.' The agent stood up. 'I'm afraid there's not much more I can do for the act. That's what I've come to tell you.'

Mysto went white. 'Give us another chance, Mr. Bartlett. Look – I'm working on a new illusion – the Electric Chair. Just watch this.' He stripped off his Arab gown and sat in his vest in the crude contraption he had made. 'Right, Edna,' he called to his wife. 'Strap me in.'

Bartlett sat resignedly while the thin girl fumbled with the straps and wired up the electric connections. She smiled nervously at him as Mysto yelled at her. The agent smiled back. She was quite pretty under her make-up and he felt sorry for her. Mysto declared himself ready. He sat bound by wrists, ankles and neck to the chair and a lamp was fixed into a socket behind his head. 'Now, when Edna throws that switch, a current of 30,000 volts enters my body and yet I come out alive.'

'Just a minute,' said Bartlett, alarmed. 'You can't . . .'

Edna threw the switch and sparks flew in every direction. The shock sent Mysto and the chair backwards across the room. Fortunately the movement broke the connection and with the aid of the stage manager and a trio of acrobats from the next dressing-room, the illusionist was freed.

At the hospital they said he was not too badly burned, and a reporter who was at the casualty ward on another job interviewed him for the local paper. The editor, amused at the story of the unsuccessful illusionist, gave it more prominence than he might normally have done. 'Miracle man survives 30,000 volt electric shock' said the headline on page three, alongside a photograph of Mysto in bed wrapped in bandages. Other papers, looking for light relief from the more ominous news, seized on the story. Mysto was beginning to make a name for himself.

On release from hospital he was tempted into trying more spectacular stunts, all of which failed, to the delight of the Press. He was fired across the Thames in a cannon and had to be rescued from drowning ten feet from the bank. He was buried six feet under Clapham Common in a coffin and declared he would stay there for a whole week. After twenty minutes he was dug up, blue in the face, something having gone wrong with his secret breathing tube.

Goon on a Flight of Fancy

'Floppo tries again' laughed the Press as Mysto prepared to leap from Beachy Head in a home-made glider. Coast guards posed at his bedside as he lay with both legs in traction, wiggling the fingers of his left hand at the camera. Everything else was in plaster. In all the photographs, sometimes obscured by somebody else's shoulder, his wife smiled nervously in the background.

Only the outbreak of World War II stopped him from jumping from the Eiffel Tower. The war forced him from the headlines and the public lost interest.

Bartlett went into the Army and after the war became very successful as an impresario. He had forgotten Mysto completely until one day in Sydney, where he had gone to negotiate a contract, he received a call from a Mrs. Lightfoot. At first the name meant nothing, but when he heard the voice he recognised it as Edna's. She asked if he would like to have tea with her, and out of compassion he agreed. The address she gave surprised him. She lived in the exclusive Rose Bay district and Bartlett's eyebrows went up even further when the door of the expensive house was opened by a maid, who ushered him into the drawing-room. When Edna came into the room, he had an even greater surprise. Gone was the skinny, mousy-haired girl of the past and in her place stood a cool, beautifully-dressed blonde with a well-preserved figure.

She smiled at the look on Bartlett's face. 'Times have changed, haven't they? Before you ask, Arthur – poor old Mysto – has been dead for twenty years now. That's what killed him.' She pointed to a rifle framed in a case over the magnificent fireplace. 'Sit down. I'll fill you in on the gaps.'

Over sandwiches and tea served from a solid silver tea service, she began to talk. 'Arthur never made it again after the war. Nobody wanted to know him, so he came out to Australia. Times were hard to start with and we settled down in Western New South Wales. Arthur got a job selling cars and kept his hand in doing odd concerts for charity. Then one day he happened to show his old press cuttings to a man on the town's newspaper. They were looking for something to boost circulation and Arthur said that he'd do a trick that hadn't been pulled for years – the stunt that killed Ching Lung Soo at Wood Green Empire.'

'Catching a bullet in his teeth?' Bartlett was incredulous. He looked at the rifle on the wall.

'Oh, Arthur said he knew how it was done – that Ching Lung Soo had neglected to take precautions and that the trick was foolproof. "All it means," he said to me, "is that you have two chambers in the rifle. In the top one you put the bullet, and underneath there's a second secret chamber filled with powder which fires a blank cartridge when the trigger's pulled. The gun goes off but the bullet stays where it is. Beforehand the bullet is marked by an independent witness and that's the one I palm, replacing it in the rifle with an ordinary unmarked bullet. I put the marked one in my mouth and that's the one I spit out on the silver tray you hand me after the gun goes off – there's nothing to it."

'I pleaded with him to change his mind. But no, he was determined to go through with it.' She pushed back a wisp of blonde hair that had strayed from her careful coiffure. 'At least, I said to him, think of me for a change. Take out an insurance policy in case anything goes wrong. "Who's going to pay the premium?" he said in that bloody irritating whine of his. "Get the newspaper people to take it out in my name. They're the ones who are sponsoring you."

'To cut a long story short, they insured him for £100,000 after making absolutely sure that nothing could go wrong. Of course they knew how the trick worked and the rifle was never out of their hands until the day of the stunt. It was a lovely day, I remember. Arthur had a special black velvet cloak made for the occasion, though I had to put up with my old sequinned leotard and tights – the mean bugger. There was a big turn-out, practically the whole town was there. Photographers from all over New South Wales came along and Arthur was in his element again.

'Everything went as planned. He got the Mayor to mark the bullet and he palmed it without managing to drop it. Then he slipped it in his mouth as I stood in front of him to put the blindfold on. The marksman put the rifle to his shoulder. Arthur spread out his arms, showing the lovely red lining of his cloak, and took a deep breath. The crowd held it with him. You could feel the tension in the air.' She crossed her legs elegantly and took another sip.

Bartlett leaned forward intently.

She put down the cup. '"Ready," Arthur shouted. The gun fired and I stepped up with the silver tray for him to spit out the bullet on, but he crumpled and fell forward on his face. He died within seconds.'

Bartlett looked into Edna's eyes for a long time, saying nothing. She met his stare with assurance and he was forced to look away. He inclined his head towards the rifle on the wall.

Edna shook her head. 'I know what you're thinking,' she said. 'That insurance policy, this house, the lovely furniture and me and Arthur always quarrelling. I got the money, granted, but you're wrong. I had nothing to do with his death. The bullet killed him all right. When he shouted "Ready", he swallowed it and choked himself on the thing.' She smiled sweetly. 'He never did get a trick right.'

She held up the silver teapot. 'I see you've drunk all your tea – you must have a big swallow. Arthur had such a tiny throat.'

Appeal on Behalf of the EPNS Society

I WOULD LIKE to make a plea for the preservation of the fast-dwindling art of spoon playing. For too long the clatter of a well-played pair of spoons has been missing from the musical scene, and I intend to do something about it. I have formed the EPNS Society – the initials standing for Educating the Public in the Noble art of Spoon playing.

It is the ideal leisure occupation for young and old. Start the youngsters off at the age of three or so with egg spoons and work up the scale to the serving spoon, suzophone of the cutlery orchestra. There was a cook I knew in the army who could play a chorus of 'Sweet Sue' on a pair of ladles. Unfortunately he over-reached himself one night in the NAAFI and crushed three fingers. Of course, he was an exception, and to get the best possible tone and fluidity of movement one should use soup spoons. The method of playing is to hold the spoons firmly in the hand, back to back, with one finger supporting the handles and a gap of about a quarter of an inch between the heads. They are then struck smartly against the hand or any other part of the anatomy, producing a percussive effect. The skilful manipulator can run his spoons up his arm, where the corrugation of the sleeve gives an attractive stuttering sound, and then glide gracefully off the elbow on to the knee without once losing a beat. An aquaintance of mine never fails to bring tears to my eyes with his performance of Ketèlbey's 'In a Monastery Garden' using only teaspoons and accompanying himself throughout with impressions of bird song. Talent of this kind is increasingly hard to find.

I would like to see the art taught in schools and the humble spoon raised to its proper status amongst the world's great instruments. Let's have another LSO – the London Spoon Orchestra. Why not sell all our army band instruments and replace them with spoons? We might even save enough money at the Ministry of Defence to enable us to stay on in the abandoned outposts of our Empire. Picture the massed bands of Her Majesty's Brigade of Guards clattering proudly as they swing down the Mall. That would give the Chinese something to think about – they could never achieve the same effect with chop sticks.

Between numbers there's an interesting little party-piece one can perform with a spoon. Rest your fist on the table, place the back of a spoon before it and allow the thumb to work up and down over the first two knuckles. You now have a pretty good impression of a fat lady taking a bath. All good clean fun, and yet another facet of the spoon as an instrument of entertainment.

If you would like to send £2 to me, care of the East Acton Spoon Manufacturing Company, East Acton, you will receive a pair of soup spoons specially engraved with our Society's initials, EPNS, and a copy of 'Bye Bye Blues' orchestrated for spoons. Between us we can make the sound of British spoons rattle around the world. Uri Geller need not apply.

A Man Must Do What He Has To Do . . .

He grew as no one else I knew,
Not up – but sideways out,
Until he could conceal a view
Or blot a landscape out.
He's met his doom, no time for gloom,
Let's all take off our hats,
For where he stood we'll now have room
To build a block of flats.

This tribute to his late friend Harry Secombe was written by Terence A. Milligan, arch conservationist (Marble Arch and Admiralty Arch to name but a few) and Poet Laureate. He has since been asked to resign.

Before going into the bizarre nature of Secombe's passing, it is necessary to look at the man behind the performer, to examine the little-known facts of his childhood and his surprising army career.

He was born in 1921 in Swansea, South Wales to a Mr. and Mrs. Secombe, from whom he took his name. As soon as he was able to read he developed a taste for the romantic novel, and the works of Anthony Hope, Sir Walter Scott and Elinor Glyn were his constant bedtime companions. At the age of twelve he discovered in the mirror what he thought was a strawberry birthmark and for some months secretly believed that he had been left as a baby on the doorstep of 6, Dan-y-Graig Terrace by impoverished Russian royalty. This illusion was dispelled when his mother found him inspecting the mark very intently one warm afternoon and revealed, between cuffs, that he had been trapped by a falling toilet seat at the age of three.

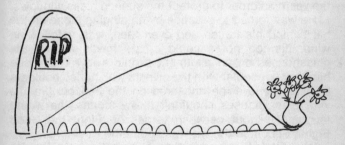

The first signs of Secombe the creative artist appeared when his parents acquired a gramophone. He took to leaping around the house to the music, wearing the boots the doctor had suggested as a support for his weak ankles. He also took to wearing lampshades and his mother's hats. His parents exchanged worried looks, and one day his father presented him with a pair of boxing gloves. He put them on his head.

His scholastic achievements were few. Overshadowed by a brilliant elder brother and a clever four-year-old sister he turned instead to sport. He was caught carving his initials on his desk during a maths lesson, and told by the master that he was for the high jump. He won the event easily and followed it up with a superb win in the three-legged race, from which he was subsequently disqualified when it was realised that he was running alone.

Perhaps the turning point in his life came when he joined the church choir. Secombe was attracted by the uniform of surplice and cassock and his innate sense of theatre developed rapidly as he assisted in the ancient rites of the services. He revelled in the old hymns, forever striving to sing higher and louder than anyone else. In this he succeeded so well that his solos in the church concerts were performed from behind locked doors in the vestry in order to protect the stained glass windows.

He was forced to practice hymn singing alone on the hill behind his house and even then, with a following wind, his top notes could create havoc among the glasshouses on an allotment a mile away. This made him very unpopular with the owners who hurled boulders at him whenever he appeared on the horizon. 'People with glass houses shouldn't throw stones,' he would laughingly shout between verses of 'Fight the Good Fight'. Secombe the wit was beginning to emerge.

World War II arrived in time to save the situation. He was called up with the T.A., to the delight of the neighbours who formed the first Adolf Hitler fan club in war-time Britain.

His army career was undistinguished until he was sent to North Africa in 1942, an event which changed the whole course of the war. The story has never been revealed until now for security reasons, but it throws an interesting light on his sudden departure from this life yesterday evening.

'I was at a troop concert in Tunisia in December 1942,' said Major General Sir Brian Cobblers at his home last night, 'when this little fat Lance Bombardier came on stage. He did some rather unfunny impressions and then he began to sing. My God, I'd never heard anything like it. Windows broke, and men dived for cover as his top notes shattered the glasses in the Officers' Mess. I sat there deafened by the noise, and then suddenly it came to me – why not harness this terrible power, turn it against the enemy and get myself a K.B.E.?

'That night we drove Secombe out into the desert and placed him in a large round hole immediately in front of an Italian Division, with instructions to begin singing 'O Sole Mio' at 4.30 a.m. My Staff Captain and I retreated to a safe distance, put in our ear-plugs and waited for zero hour. Bang on the dot he burst into song – so loudly that even with protection our ears rang.

'For two or three mintues there was no reaction at all from the other side, then pandemonium broke out. White flags waved, men reeled about clutching their heads and sobbing piteously. "Please-a-stop," cried the Italian Commander brokenly. "We-give-a-in." My strategy had worked. Secombe the Sonic Songster Mark I was born, and under conditions of great secrecy we used him again and again throughout Europe. Believe me, if he hadn't developed laryngitis at Arnhem we would have been in Berlin in 1944. Can't believe he's dead. Still, a man must do what he has to do.'

After the end of the war Secombe drifted into show business, managing to control his voice to reasonably bearable proportions, though he was still determined to hit the highest note ever recorded. At one performance at Blackpool Opera House he unleashed a top C which opened the swing bridge at Warrington.

Success of a sort came his way – he acquired a wife, an agent and four children, though not necessarily in

Goon on a Flight of Fancy

that order. He was written up in the popular papers and written down in the intellectual ones. He suffered fools gladly because he was one of them, and like all entertainers he was basically insecure. This was to be expected from someone who once said of his career that it was 'built on such shaky foundations as a high-pitched giggle, a raspberry and a sprinkling of top C's'.

He vowed to retire on his seventieth birthday, and on the same day to achieve his still unfulfilled ambition. Yesterday, September 8th, was his date with destiny. Gently brushing aside the protestations of his family with the words 'A man must do what he has to do', he went alone into the Albert Hall, which he had hired that evening for his attempt on the highest recorded note in history. The silent crowd outside had not long to wait. From within came a sound which started low then gradually got higher and higher and louder and louder until the very ground began to shake. It soared to an unbelievable height and stayed there, shimmering in the evening air. There was a second's silence and then slowly, as in a dream, the Albert Hall collapsed inwards.

They found him under the rubble barely conscious, and with only minutes to live he tried to speak. 'Shh,' they said, 'we know – a man must do what he has to do. And you've done it.'

'Yes,' he whispered before his head dropped forward, 'and the toilet seat fell on me.'

A memorial service is to be held at the London Palladium. There will be no singing.